Truth, Peace, and Faith

Truth, Peace, and Faith

Sergiu Margan

RESOURCE *Publications* • Eugene, Oregon

TRUTH, PEACE, AND FAITH

Copyright © 2025 Sergiu Margan. All rights reserved. Except for brief quotations in critical publications or reviews, no part of this book may be reproduced in any manner without prior written permission from the publisher. Write: Permissions, Wipf and Stock Publishers, 199 W. 8th Ave., Suite 3, Eugene, OR 97401.

Resource Publications
An Imprint of Wipf and Stock Publishers
199 W. 8th Ave., Suite 3
Eugene, OR 97401

www.wipfandstock.com

PAPERBACK ISBN: 979-8-3852-6225-0
HARDCOVER ISBN: 979-8-3852-6226-7
EBOOK ISBN: 979-8-3852-6227-4
VERSION NUMBER 10/21/25

Scripture quotations from the Bible are taken from The Holy Bible, New International Version®, NIV®. Copyright © 2011 by Biblica, Inc. Used with permission of Zondervan. All rights reserved worldwide. www.zondervan.com.

Scripture quotations from the Qur'an are taken from The Qur'an, trans. M. A. S. Abdel Haleem (Oxford: Oxford University Press, 2008).

To Andrea, my beloved wife—
my steadfast companion and undeserved grace.
I am endlessly grateful for your life beside mine.

To our children, Bella and Luca—
blessings from God—your laughter and wonder
keep my heart awake to his goodness.

Contents

Preface | xi

1 Jerusalem—The Heart of Conflict | 1
2 The Jewish Temples—Rise and Fall | 3
3 Islam's Claim and the Al-Aqsa Mosque | 5
4 The Third Temple—Prophecy, Politics, and the Point of No Return | 8
5 Jesus—The Fulfilled Promise and the Rejected Cornerstone | 12
6 The Cosmic War—God's Plan, Satan's Rebellion, and the Free Will of Man | 15
7 Jihad, Armageddon, and the Last Stand for Truth | 17
8 The Messiah Foretold—A Convergence of Faiths | 20
9 Choosing Sides—Israel's Role and Humanity's Reckoning | 23
10 The Valley of Dry Bones—The Return of Israel | 26
11 The Temple Mount—A Ground Zero of Faith and Fury | 28
12 Messiah vs. Mahdi—The Battle for Divine Authority | 31
13 The Last Temple and the Return of the King | 34
14 Signs in the East—Persia, Prophecy, and the Powers Behind the Curtain | 37
15 The False Singularity—When Unity Becomes a Lie | 40

Contents

16 The Spirit and the Bride Say, "Come"—The Role of the Church Before the End | 45
17 The Nations Rage—Global Politics and the Prophecies of God | 51
18 The Final War—Truth vs. Deception | 56
19 The Garden, the Serpent, and the Origins of Evil | 61
20 Divine Intelligence—Outsmarting Evil | 63
21 The Tree of Life—Lost and Found | 66
22 The Great Encounter—When Satan Met Jesus | 70
23 The Test of Life—Reflections of God in Human Systems | 74
24 Designed or Evolved? Unmasking the Myth of Human Evolution | 78
25 The Real Intelligence—Outsmarting Evil | 84
26 The Garden Test—Why Was Lucifer Allowed In? | 86
27 The Unseen Realm—Where Does Lucifer Operate? | 89
28 When the Heavens Open—The Second Coming of Christ | 92
29 Truth Denied—The Greatest Rebellion | 95
30 The Final Invitation and the Narrow Road | 98
31 Signs of the End | 101
32 Living Like It's the Last Day | 103
33 The Philosophy of Love | 105
34 Designed for Eternity | 107
35 When the End Is Near | 108
36 Love in a World Gone Cold | 110
37 The Prophets of Our Time | 112
38 The Judgment to Come | 114
39 The Purpose Beyond the Grave | 115
40 The Eternal Battle for the Soul | 117
41 The God Who Waits | 119
42 The Faith of a Child | 122
43 Hell—The Justice No One Wants | 124

Contents

44　The Final Proof—Jesus in History and Eternity | 126
45　The Calling and the Commission | 130
46　The Road Ahead—What Will You Choose? | 132

Final Appendices and Reader Tools | 135
Bibliography | 139

Preface

JERUSALEM—NO OTHER CITY ON earth holds such profound significance and has seen such enduring conflict. To believers and nonbelievers alike, it's astonishing that this small stretch of land, scarcely larger than a metropolitan city, has been at the heart of global religious, political, and military tensions for thousands of years. The city is revered by Judaism, Christianity, and Islam, each attributing sacred and prophetic importance to its sites, especially the Temple Mount. Here, the deep-rooted desires of Jews to rebuild their Third Temple clash dramatically with Muslims determined to protect the revered Al-Aqsa Mosque and Dome of the Rock. At the intersection of faith and geopolitics, Jerusalem symbolizes a cosmic battle—one between good and evil, God and Lucifer—manifesting in human conflicts throughout history. This book delves into the intricacies of this enduring struggle, exploring how past prophecies, religious expectations, and modern geopolitics collide in a battle that seems destined to persist until prophetic fulfillment.

1

Jerusalem
The Heart of Conflict

JERUSALEM IS A CITY like no other, uniquely positioned at the crossroads of history, religion, and global politics. Throughout its millennia-long existence, it has witnessed unparalleled strife, deep devotion, and profound spiritual revelations, making it an epicenter of both unity and division.

Historically, Jerusalem has been the center of empires, conquests, and crusades. Its earliest recorded history places it as a Canaanite city-state, evolving through eras of Israelite kings, Babylonian captivity, Persian restoration, Hellenistic influences, Roman occupation, Byzantine Christianity, Islamic conquest, Crusader kingdoms, Ottoman rule, British mandate, and finally, the modern state of Israel. Each era left an indelible mark on Jerusalem, contributing layers of cultural and religious significance.

The city's sacred geography makes it uniquely contentious. The Temple Mount stands as the most intensely disputed piece of real estate on earth. To Jews, it is Mount Moriah, the site of Solomon's Temple and its successor, where the divine presence once dwelled and where prophetic visions of a future Third Temple still captivate Jewish imaginations and hopes. For Muslims, the same ground is Al-Haram al-Sharif, the Noble Sanctuary housing

Al-Aqsa Mosque and the Dome of the Rock, from where the prophet Muhammad is believed to have ascended into heaven during the night journey (Q 17:1).

Christian reverence for Jerusalem is equally profound, centered on the life, death, and resurrection of Jesus Christ. Sites such as the Church of the Holy Sepulchre and the Mount of Olives draw countless pilgrims, further amplifying the city's global significance.

Geopolitically, the city's strategic location has consistently placed it at the nexus of major conflicts and alliances. The establishment of Israel in 1948 and subsequent Arab-Israeli wars, notably in 1948, 1967, and 1973, reinforced Jerusalem's status as a contentious international issue. Internationally contested sovereignty and diplomatic disputes over its capital status perpetuate its central role in global politics.

Yet, Jerusalem's significance transcends politics and warfare—it symbolizes deeper spiritual battles, serving as a tangible manifestation of the cosmic struggle between forces of good and evil. This struggle is not merely symbolic; it has real-world implications, shaping international policies, fueling regional tensions, and influencing millions around the globe.

This chapter lays the foundational understanding necessary to grasp why Jerusalem, despite its modest geographical footprint, continually occupies a pivotal role in global affairs. By unpacking the historical, religious, and geopolitical complexities, we begin to understand how one city can command such unparalleled attention and passion, setting the stage for deeper explorations in subsequent chapters.

2

The Jewish Temples

Rise and Fall

JERUSALEM'S IDENTITY AND SIGNIFICANCE are intimately tied to the rise and fall of its ancient temples, structures of profound religious importance for Judaism and symbols of a covenant between God and his chosen people.

The First Temple, built by King Solomon around the tenth century BCE on Mount Moriah, was intended as a permanent dwelling place for God's divine presence. It housed the ark of the covenant, symbolizing God's promise and presence among the Israelites. This temple was the focal point of religious and national identity, but in 586 BCE, the Babylonians destroyed it, leading the Jewish people into exile. This catastrophic event shaped Jewish theology and national consciousness profoundly.[1]

The Second Temple emerged after the Babylonian exile, completed in 516 BCE under Persian authorization. It stood through periods of Persian, Greek, and Roman dominance, becoming an even more significant religious and cultural center. However, the Second Temple met a violent end in 70 CE during a brutal Roman siege, following the Jewish revolt. Its destruction fulfilled several

---

1. Bruce, *Israel and the Nations*.

prophecies and deeply affected Jewish spiritual life, precipitating centuries of diaspora and longing.

Central to understanding these temples is the figure of Jesus Christ. In his ministry, Jesus prophesied the destruction of the temple and its symbolic rebuilding in three days, a reference to his death and resurrection. This prophecy, misunderstood initially, became clear after his crucifixion, resurrection, and the Romans' eventual destruction of the physical temple.

The memory and significance of these temples remain alive in Jewish consciousness, fueling the dream and religious imperative to build a Third Temple. The Third Temple holds immense messianic significance, believed by many Jews to herald the arrival of the Messiah and a new era of divine favor and peace.

Furthermore, God's incarnation through Jesus represents the ultimate covenant between God and humanity—a truth that many Jews have historically rejected. Despite evidence of Jesus fulfilling messianic prophecies, the Jewish people have endured immense suffering over millennia, clinging to hope for a Messiah who would save exclusively them. Ironically, God Almighty offered salvation to the entire world through Christ, not just to a single group. Examining this resistance, we must question why Jewish belief diverged so significantly from the original teachings of Abraham, Moses, and David. Why have they dismissed compelling evidence? When will this long-held belief evolve? Ultimately, Christians find themselves dependent on the Jewish presence as a barrier against Islamic expansion, yet the Jewish people remain unaware or resistant to their critical yet precarious role in this cosmic conflict destined to climax dramatically.

3

Islam's Claim and the Al-Aqsa Mosque

THE ISLAMIC CONNECTION TO Jerusalem, particularly the Al-Aqsa Mosque, introduces an additional layer of complexity to the city's already intricate religious and geopolitical landscape.

Following Muhammad's night journey (Isra and Mi'raj), Jerusalem gained immense significance within Islam, becoming its third-holiest city after Mecca and Medina. According to Islamic tradition, the prophet Muhammad miraculously journeyed overnight from Mecca to Jerusalem and ascended to heaven from the site known as Al-Haram al-Sharif, now the location of Al-Aqsa Mosque and Dome of the Rock (Q 17:1).

Constructed in the late seventh century CE under the Umayyad Caliphate, Al-Aqsa Mosque symbolizes Islamic religious heritage and presence in the region. For Muslims, the mosque signifies continuity with the prophetic tradition and Islam's deep ties to the Abrahamic faiths.

Historically, Islam's expansion, including under Muhammad, involved both peaceful diplomacy and military conflict. Notably, Islamic sources and non-Islamic records document violent events such as the siege and execution of the Banu Qurayza, a Jewish tribe in Medina. While such events were not unique to Islam—medieval Christianity, Hinduism, and even Buddhist political regimes also committed acts of violence—they are often debated within theological and ethical contexts today.

In contrast to the violent elements in some Islamic histories, other world religions like Buddhism, Shintoism, Sikhism, and Hinduism have had long periods of peaceful coexistence. Yet, these faiths, too, have experienced episodes of conflict, depending on region and era. It is therefore historically imprecise to assert that Islam alone has caused widespread violence; rather, its theological-political fusion and global footprint have amplified its role in current conflicts, especially in the Middle East.

Today, Islamic stewardship of Al-Haram al-Sharif remains a cornerstone of Muslim identity, while Jewish aspirations to reclaim the Temple Mount continue to be viewed by many Muslims as existential threats. The political rivalry between Iran and Saudi Arabia, partly rooted in Sunni-Shia tensions, fuels ambitions to influence Jerusalem's future spiritual status.

Since the twentieth century, the broader Middle East has been marred by nearly continuous warfare and upheaval. Examples include:

- The Arab-Israeli wars (1948, 1956, 1967, 1973): Ongoing conflict over the existence and borders of Israel, involving Egypt, Syria, Jordan, Lebanon, and others.
- The Lebanese Civil War (1975–1990): A multifaceted war involving Muslim and Christian militias, Syrian intervention, and Israeli invasion.
- The Iran-Iraq War (1980–1988): A brutal conflict driven by religious, ethnic, and territorial disputes.
- The Gulf War (1990–1991): Iraq's invasion of Kuwait and the subsequent international response.
- The Iraq War (2003–2011): US-led invasion followed by insurgency, sectarian violence, and emergence of ISIS.

- The Syrian Civil War (2011–present): An ongoing disaster with millions displaced and hundreds of thousands killed, with deep Sunni-Alawite divides.

- The Libyan Civil Wars (2011, 2014–present): Following the fall of Gaddhafi, multiple factions, including Islamist militias, continue to battle for power.

- The Yemeni Civil War (2015–present): A humanitarian catastrophe driven by Sunni-Shia proxy war between Saudi Arabia and Iran.

- The Afghan conflicts (1979–2021): From the Soviet invasion, civil war, Taliban rule, US invasion, and eventual Taliban resurgence.

- The Egyptian Revolution and unrest (2011–2013): Political upheaval, the rise and fall of the Muslim Brotherhood, followed by military rule.

No other region with such religious legacy has simultaneously seen so much bloodshed. Despite common languages, culture, and religious affiliation, Muslim-majority nations have turned on each other repeatedly, raising a profound question: Why is peace so elusive in a region that claims divine revelation? Why do faith, family, and shared heritage so often become reasons for division instead of unity?

This chapter examines Islam's historical, religious, and political claims to Jerusalem, aiming to offer a fair yet critical analysis grounded in documented events, while recognizing the broader implications for interfaith understanding and conflict.

4

The Third Temple
Prophecy, Politics, and the Point of No Return

THE IDEA OF A Third Temple is not merely theological—it is prophetic, political, and potentially explosive. In Jewish eschatology, the rebuilding of the temple is not just an aspiration; it is a divine imperative tied to the coming of the Messiah and the full restoration of Israel. This dream, however, directly collides with Muslim control over the Temple Mount.

Orthodox Jews believe that the Third Temple will be built in the Messianic age and that its construction is essential for the fulfillment of God's covenant with Israel. Groups like the Temple Institute in Jerusalem actively research and prepare articles, vessels, and priestly garments for this future construction. Some believe the temple must be built before the Messiah comes; others believe the Messiah will rebuild it himself.

The dilemma, however, is that the Dome of the Rock currently occupies the exact location where the Jewish temple once stood. For Muslims, removing it would be unthinkable. For Jews, rebuilding the temple anywhere else is unacceptable. This immovable theological impasse has placed the world on a prophetic knife's edge.

Politically, the notion of rebuilding the temple is already stirring unrest. Israeli security forces have clashed with Muslim worshippers at the Temple Mount numerous times. Any indication of Jewish plans to alter the status quo provokes outrage throughout the Islamic world. Radical groups have threatened jihad should the temple be rebuilt. The geopolitical fallout of such an act would likely trigger a regional, if not global, crisis.

And yet, for many Christians, the rebuilding of the Third Temple is seen as a necessary step in the unfolding of end-times prophecy. According to interpretations of the book of Revelation, the antichrist will defile this temple before Christ returns to defeat him and establish his eternal kingdom. In this way, the Third Temple is not just a Jewish aspiration—it has become central to Christian eschatology as well.

This prophetic convergence has led to an unusual alliance between evangelical Christians and Orthodox Jews. Christians support Jewish sovereignty over the Temple Mount not out of theological agreement with Judaism, but because they believe it will hasten the return of Christ. This alliance, while strategic, is also precarious. Both sides see the temple as central to their vision of redemption—but the final outcomes they anticipate are radically different.

The Third Temple is no longer just a symbol of hope; it is a flash point of prophecy and power. The world watches Jerusalem with nervous anticipation, knowing that if the foundation stones of a Third Temple are ever laid, it will mark the crossing of a spiritual and political Rubicon.

HISTORICAL AND PHILOSOPHICAL EVALUATION OF THE TEMPLE MOUNT CONFLICT

Did Muhammad or Islam intentionally claim Mount Moriah?

This question—though rarely raised—is both valid and historically grounded. Mount Moriah was considered sacred to the Jewish people more than two thousand years before the rise of Islam. It was the site of the First and Second Temples, and its religious centrality is uncontested across ancient Jewish, Roman, Greek, and Christian sources.

The Dome of the Rock was constructed in 691 CE by the Umayyad Caliph Abd al-Malik, decades after Muhammad's death in 632 CE. It was built on the Temple Mount, the most sacred ground in Judaism, and framed theologically through an Islamic tradition that interpreted Muhammad's night journey (Isra and Mi'raj) as culminating at this location. However, Jerusalem is not directly named in the Qur'an as the destination of the night journey—it only refers to "Al-Masjid al-Aqsa" (the farthest mosque). Early Islamic commentators retrospectively equated this phrase with Jerusalem (Q 17:1).

This retroactive interpretation has led many historians to conclude that strategic and political motives were involved in the choice of Mount Moriah. At the time of construction, rival factions controlled Mecca and Medina. Elevating Jerusalem as an Islamic center allowed the Umayyad Caliphate to solidify religious authority while competing with Christian and Jewish traditions. It was a powerful symbolic and theological statement—but it also entrenched centuries of conflict.

No other religion in history has claimed the most sacred site of another as its own and erected holy structures on top of it with such long-term political and military consequences. Philosophically, it raises the question, Can a religion that claims peace justify such an act of dominance? If peace and respect for others are central to any faith, then the intentional overlap of religious claims on the Temple Mount seems more designed to provoke than reconcile.

While Muhammad himself did not order the building of a mosque there, the subsequent interpretation of his vision—and the deliberate architectural and political decisions that followed—secured an unresolvable flash point. The enduring conflict that arose from this decision is not just territorial—it is theological, historical, and moral.

This analysis does not aim to vilify, but to clarify. History must be confronted with honesty. Recognizing these truths helps believers of all faiths understand the complexity of the conflict and

The Third Temple

the urgent need for a deeper spiritual reckoning in the pursuit of lasting peace.

5

Jesus

The Fulfilled Promise and the Rejected Cornerstone

THE ROLE OF JESUS in this eternal conflict is both foundational and often misunderstood. Christians believe that Jesus Christ is the fulfillment of the Law and the Prophets—a divine intervention in human history through whom God established a new covenant. His life, death, and resurrection are not only central to Christianity but also deeply relevant to the question of the temple, Jerusalem, and Israel's destiny.

When Jesus said, "Destroy this temple, and in three days I will raise it up," he was speaking of his body (John 2:19–21). This declaration, misunderstood by the religious leaders of his time, pointed to a greater truth: Jesus was the new temple, the place where God meets humanity. In him, the divine presence was no longer limited to stone and sacrifice, but extended through grace and truth to the entire world (John 2:19).

The crucifixion of Jesus was not merely a Roman execution; it was the climax of prophetic history. The veil in the temple tore from top to bottom at his death (Matt 27:51), symbolizing the end of the old sacrificial system and the opening of direct access to God through Christ. His resurrection three days later was the ultimate sign that he is who he claimed to be: the Son of God, the Savior of the world.

Yet, the irony remains profound: the very people through whom God brought the Messiah largely rejected him. As prophesied in Ps 118:22, "The stone the builders rejected has become the cornerstone." This rejection continues today. Many in the Jewish community still await a messiah, unaware that he has already come. Their suffering, exile, and persecution throughout history seem tied not only to external enemies but also to a spiritual blindness foretold by Isaiah (Isa 6:9-10).

This rejection, however, is not the end of the story. Paul the apostle affirms in Rom 11 that a time will come when the Jewish people will recognize their Messiah. The Christian calling is not to condemn the Jews but to pray for their eyes to be opened and to recognize the spiritual foundation they helped lay.

Meanwhile, the role of Jesus in Islamic theology adds another layer of complexity. Muslims regard Jesus (Isa) as a prophet and the Messiah, born of the Virgin Mary, and a miracle worker—but not divine. Islam denies the crucifixion and resurrection, seeing his ascension as an escape from death. This contradiction creates an irreconcilable theological divide between Christianity and Islam regarding the meaning of salvation.

Jesus stands at the center of this conflict—not as a figure of war, but of peace. He is the bridge between heaven and earth, between the old covenant and the new. His teachings on love, mercy, and sacrifice present a radical contrast to the political and religious hostilities centered on Jerusalem.

What, then, is the historical basis for the life and teachings of Jesus? The New Testament Gospels—Matthew, Mark, Luke, and John—are widely regarded by historians as early, eyewitness-based accounts. Paul's epistles, written within two decades of Jesus's death, testify to his crucifixion and resurrection. Roman historians such as Tacitus and Jewish historians like Josephus also mention Jesus of Nazareth as a real figure who was crucified under Pontius Pilate.[1]

---

1. Tacitus, *Annals*; Josephus, *Jewish Antiquities*.

Truth, Peace, and Faith

Archaeological discoveries such as the Pilate stone (discovered in Caesarea Maritima) and the Dead Sea Scrolls (confirming textual consistency of Old Testament prophecies) reinforce the reliability of both the context and the content of Scripture. The consistency and rapid spread of early Christian testimony—despite intense persecution and martyrdom—support the view that the disciples truly believed what they proclaimed: that Jesus rose from the dead.

Perhaps most striking is the testimony of Sir Lionel Alfred Luckhoo, a British barrister and diplomat, who holds the world record for the most consecutive legal acquittals (245 murder cases). After investigating the historical evidence for Jesus Christ with the rigorous standards of courtroom logic, he concluded, "I say unequivocally that the evidence for the resurrection of Jesus Christ is so overwhelming that it compels acceptance by proof which leaves absolutely no room for doubt."[2] His conclusion was not the result of emotional persuasion but of logical scrutiny—examining the accounts, eyewitnesses, and historical corroboration.

This chapter calls for a deeper recognition: the Messiah has come. The world's refusal to accept this fact—whether through Jewish longing for another or Islamic denial of his death—is the spiritual fuel that sustains the unrest. Peace will not come through treaties or walls, but through the Prince of Peace, who once entered Jerusalem on a donkey and will one day return as King.

The eternal conflict will continue until this truth is accepted not just by individuals but by nations. The cornerstone once rejected will again become the foundation—this time not just of a city, but of a new heaven and new earth.

---

2. Luckhoo, *Life After Death*, 64.

6

The Cosmic War

*God's Plan, Satan's Rebellion,
and the Free Will of Man*

BENEATH THE SURFACE OF world events lies a deeper war—one not fought with armies or weapons, but with truth and lies, light and darkness, freedom and bondage. It is the cosmic war between God and Satan, between the Creator of heaven and earth and the adversary who once dwelled among angels.

The Bible reveals that Satan, formerly known as Lucifer, was a high-ranking angel who rebelled against God out of pride (Isa 14:12–15; Ezek 28:12–17). He sought to exalt himself above the throne of God. Cast down from heaven, he became the deceiver, the accuser, and the enemy of all that is holy. Yet his rebellion did not end there—he waged war on humanity, God's image-bearers, seeking to corrupt, enslave, and destroy.

When Adam and Eve chose to disobey God in Eden, they exercised their God-given free will, but also opened the door to sin and death. Humanity became ensnared in the devil's scheme, caught in a cycle of rebellion, violence, and spiritual blindness. However, God did not abandon his creation. From the beginning, he laid out a redemptive plan that culminated in Jesus Christ—the Son of God who would crush the serpent's head (Gen 3:15).

This cosmic war is not abstract. It explains why the world is filled with injustice, deception, and unending conflict. Satan's influence is not just spiritual—it manifests in ideologies, false religions, corrupt governments, and oppressive systems. He even tried to tempt Jesus by offering him the kingdoms of the world in exchange for worship (Matt 4:8–10)—a clear admission that he held sway over them.

But God is not passive. Throughout history, he has raised up prophets, kings, and messengers to reveal truth, uphold justice, and prepare the way for his ultimate intervention. Jesus was not merely a prophet or a moral teacher—he was God in the flesh, sent to defeat Satan, not by violence, but through sacrificial love.

At the cross, Jesus disarmed the spiritual powers of darkness (Col 2:15). His resurrection declared the enemy defeated and secured the future restoration of all things. Yet until that final day, the conflict rages on. Believers are called to be soldiers of light (Eph 6:12–13), resisting deception and standing firm in truth.

The gift of free will remains central. God desires love that is freely chosen, not coerced. Every person must decide—will they follow the Prince of Peace or the father of lies? There is no middle ground.

This chapter helps frame the theological and philosophical foundation for understanding the visible chaos in the world today. Behind every war, every division, and every spiritual confusion lies an ancient enemy. But behind every act of truth, sacrifice, and redemption stands the eternal King.

We are living not in an age of random disorder, but of decisive battle. The end has been written. Satan's time is short, and his desperation is great. Yet God's power is greater still—and his plan is unfolding just as foretold.

7

Jihad, Armageddon, and the Last Stand for Truth

IN BOTH ISLAMIC AND Christian eschatology, the end times are marked by global upheaval, spiritual deception, and an ultimate battle between good and evil. Nowhere is this more clearly expressed than in the concept of jihad and the prophecy of Armageddon.

In Islam, jihad is often misunderstood. While it can denote personal spiritual struggle, history shows that the term has also been used to justify violent expansion, conquest, and holy war. Radical interpretations of jihad have been used by extremist movements across the Middle East to incite wars and justify terror. Groups like Al-Qaeda, ISIS, and Hezbollah invoke Islamic texts to claim religious legitimacy for global warfare against non-Muslims and even against fellow Muslims.

In Christianity, the battle of Armageddon is described in the book of Revelation as the final clash between the forces of Satan and the returning Christ. This conflict, centered around Jerusalem, involves the armies of the world gathering to oppose God. Yet in this climactic moment, Jesus returns—not as the suffering servant, but as the conquering King—to defeat evil once and for all (Rev 19:11–21).

The striking parallel is that both world religions anticipate a final apocalyptic battle. Yet only Christianity describes the Messiah personally intervening, judging the nations, and ushering in everlasting peace. Islam anticipates Jesus returning, but under its framework, he submits to Islamic law and assists in the establishment of a global Islamic order—again, contradicting his original gospel and teachings of grace.

This theological divergence creates an irreconcilable vision for the end. One sees Christ establishing peace through judgment and resurrection power; the other sees him enforcing a system he never taught.

A significant contradiction also arises from within Islamic theology regarding Jesus. Passages in the Qur'an acknowledge Jesus's virgin birth (Q 3:45–47), his sinlessness, and most astonishingly, his ability to create life. In Q 3:49 and 5:110, Jesus is said to have shaped a bird from clay and breathed into it, and it became alive—"by the permission of Allah." No other prophet in the Bible or Qur'an is described as giving life to the dead or creating life from clay. The implication is profound: if giving life is a divine act (as reserved for God alone elsewhere in the Qur'an), how can one attribute this to a mere prophet and yet deny his divinity?

This contradiction raises fundamental questions: Can the one who creates life from lifelessness not be God? Is it logically consistent to credit a prophet with divine powers and yet insist he is not divine? Even within the Qur'anic framework, this creates an unresolved theological tension.

Current geopolitics reflect these eschatological tensions. The rise of Iranian nuclear ambitions, Sunni-Shia rivalries, the Israeli-Palestinian conflict, and radical Islamic groups' obsession with Jerusalem all point to a spiritual powder keg. Iran has openly stated its desire to usher in the Mahdi (Islamic messianic figure) through global chaos, while Israel's very existence continues to provoke regional hostility.

Jihad, Armageddon, and the Last Stand for Truth

As the world moves closer to this prophetic climax, Christians are called to discernment. The rise of global deception, moral decay, and anti-Christian sentiment are not coincidental—they are signs of a greater spiritual conflict building toward a divine resolution.

Jesus warned of false prophets, wars, and persecution. But he also promised, "When you see these things, lift up your heads, for your redemption is drawing near" (Luke 21:28).

This chapter serves as a warning and a call: the battle lines are forming. The war is not just military or ideological—it is spiritual. The armies of this world may gather in the valley of decision, but victory belongs to the Lamb.

8

The Messiah Foretold
A Convergence of Faiths

THROUGHOUT HISTORY, THE IDEA of a coming savior—one who will bring justice, peace, and divine truth—has appeared in the scriptures and traditions of many cultures. The Hebrew Bible speaks of a Messiah who will redeem Israel and establish God's kingdom. Christianity proclaims Jesus as that Messiah, fulfilled in his first coming and returning in glory. Islam also awaits the return of Isa (Jesus), though within a very different framework.

The convergence of these messianic expectations is both profound and perilous. Each tradition believes in a central figure of ultimate deliverance, yet they differ on identity, nature, and mission.

In Judaism, the Messiah (Mashiach) is expected to be a political and spiritual leader, a descendant of David, who will rebuild the temple in Jerusalem, gather the Jews back to Israel, and bring peace to the world. Jews have historically rejected Jesus as this figure, primarily because he did not fulfill the political and territorial expectations associated with the Messiah. The Gospels, however, show that many of their own religious leaders—such as Nicodemus, and especially Caiaphas the high priest (John 11:49–52)—recognized Jesus's spiritual authority. Caiaphas even prophesied, though unknowingly,

The Messiah Foretold

that Jesus would die for the nation, and not for that nation only, but for all the children of God scattered abroad.

Despite their knowledge, many Jewish leaders rejected Jesus because they feared losing power and control. As stated in John 11:48, "If we let him go on like this, everyone will believe in him, and then the Romans will come and take away both our place and our nation." Their rejection was not due to lack of evidence but due to fear, pride, and political convenience.

The theological idea that God would only save one nation—Israel—is also inconsistent with God's broader message of justice and mercy through the prophets. Abraham was promised that "all nations on earth will be blessed through you" (Gen 22:18). God's love, as demonstrated throughout Scripture, has always reached beyond Israel to all humanity.

In Islam, Jesus is honored as a prophet and Messiah, but his divinity is completely rejected. While passages in the Qur'an acknowledge his virgin birth, sinlessness, miracles, and even that he gave life to clay birds (Q 3:49, 5:110), other passages simultaneously deny his crucifixion and resurrection (Q 4:157–58). This results in a severe contradiction: a man who performs divine acts, yet is not divine. Islam removes the divinity from Jesus entirely—yet assigns him roles and powers no other prophet in Islam possesses.

The claim that Jesus did not die on the cross or rise from the dead is a central tenet in Islam, yet its origin raises critical questions. This claim comes from a man, Muhammad, who said he received revelations from an angel in a cave—six hundred years after the events of Jesus's life, death, and resurrection. By contrast, the Gospel accounts were written by eyewitnesses or their close associates, mere decades after the events occurred. These records contain detailed testimony of Jesus's death, burial, empty tomb, post-resurrection appearances, and the radical transformation of his followers.

In a court of law, no judge would dismiss consistent eyewitness testimonies in favor of a single uncorroborated account given centuries later. The credibility of the gospel is grounded in the historical proximity of its sources, the willingness of the apostles to die for their testimony, and the internal consistency of the narrative. Furthermore, all of Jesus's earliest followers were Jews—men and women who would have had no reason to fabricate a new religion that broke from their deeply embedded traditions unless they were absolutely convinced it was true.

This theological distortion parallels the pattern of deception seen in the garden of Eden. There, Satan twisted God's words to offer a "truth" that led to death. In Islam, Lucifer appears to have done the same—acknowledging Jesus just enough to appear truthful, but stripping away his identity as the Son of God and the Savior of the world. The outcome is a religion with pieces of the truth, repurposed to prevent people from finding the full truth.

Thus, in both Judaism and Islam, we see two different strategies of spiritual deception: one, through fear and pride leading to rejection; the other, through partial truth masking the whole. In both cases, the result is the same—denial of the only One who can save.

This convergence of belief around one figure—Jesus—demands close examination. Why is it that the world's largest religions all point to him in some form? Why is he the most referenced and revered figure outside of their own founders? Is this not itself a clue to his uniqueness?

What makes Jesus unparalleled is not just the attention he receives, but the nature of his mission: he claimed to be the way, the truth, and the life (John 14:6). His miracles, his teachings, his death, and his resurrection stand in stark contrast to every other religious leader. No other figure claimed divinity, predicted his own death and resurrection, and then fulfilled it before hundreds of eyewitnesses.

This chapter invites readers to reflect: If all roads speak of a coming Messiah, and only one has come claiming to fulfill that role with power, humility, and eternal authority—should not the world reconsider its verdict?

The convergence of faiths around Jesus is not a call to pluralism, but a call to decision. Either he is who he said he is, or he is not. The weight of history, prophecy, and spiritual transformation testifies that he is.

9

Choosing Sides

Israel's Role and Humanity's Reckoning

GOD DECLARED TO ABRAHAM, "I will bless those who bless you, and whoever curses you I will curse; and all peoples on earth will be blessed through you" (Gen 12:3). This is echoed in the Torah and repeated throughout the Prophets. Israel was meant to be a light to the nations (Isa 42:6), a kingdom of priests (Exod 19:6), and the people through whom the Messiah would come.

Yet Israel's journey has been one of both calling and conflict. Time and again, they turned from God, suffered judgment, and were exiled. And yet, God remained faithful. The return of Israel as a nation in 1948 is not just a modern political miracle—it is a fulfillment of Ezek 37: "I will take the Israelites out of the nations where they have gone . . . and bring them back into their own land."

But with the return comes responsibility. As Jesus wept over Jerusalem, he said, "You did not recognize the time of your visitation" (Luke 19:44). The Messiah had come, and yet the majority rejected him. Still, God's plan was not thwarted. Instead, the gospel went out to the nations, and salvation was opened to all.

Now, we live in a time where the whole world is being drawn into the conflict. A passage in the Qur'an claims, "You [Muslims] are the best nation produced [as an example] for mankind" (Q

3:110), echoing Israel's own calling from Exodus. But where the Torah emphasizes righteousness and justice through covenant with God, and the gospel extends that covenant to all through Jesus, Islam redirects the center of revelation away from Jerusalem and toward Mecca. It is a battle for spiritual geography.

The world is choosing sides. Some nations rally against Israel; others support her. But the real choice is not political—it is spiritual. The Messiah has already come. The New Testament confirms that in Christ, "There is neither Jew nor Gentile . . . for you are all one in Christ Jesus" (Gal 3:28).

To ignore Jesus as Messiah is to miss the fulfillment of prophecy. To believe he was just a prophet, as Islam does, while denying his crucifixion (Q 4:157), contradicts not only Gospel witness but the testimony of countless Jewish apostles who had no reason to invent his resurrection.

The Jewish Sanhedrin feared the loss of their position (John 11:48), and the early Muslim tradition replaced the cross with a claim heard in a cave centuries later. As any court would ask—whose testimony holds more weight? Eyewitnesses of an event or someone claiming a vision long after the fact?

As this spiritual war escalates, Israel remains at the center—not because they are perfect, but because they are chosen. And Christians must recognize this battle is not just Israel's to fight. It is humanity's.

God's plan for redemption was not reactive—it was unfolding from the very beginning. From the moment of the fall in Eden, a promise was made: "He will crush your head, and you will strike his heel" (Gen 3:15). Lucifer, knowing this, worked throughout history to corrupt humanity, stop the Messiah's arrival, and derail God's purposes. Yet every act of sabotage ultimately contributed to God's victory.

Perhaps the greatest irony is this: Lucifer was defeated by his own evil. He tried to tempt Jesus in the desert (Matt 4), showing that he recognized him. He influenced Judas and the religious leaders to crucify Jesus, thinking he was eliminating the threat. But in doing so, he fulfilled the very plan that would crush him. The cross, meant as a tool of death, became the instrument of salvation.

"For the message of the cross is foolishness to those who are perishing, but to us who are being saved it is the power of God" (1 Cor 1:18). Satan's desire to destroy Christ only magnified God's glory and love.

The question remains: Will we stand with the truth of the Messiah, or fall into the deception of partial truths and historical revisionism? The time to choose is now.

10

The Valley of Dry Bones
The Return of Israel

THE RETURN OF THE nation of Israel in 1948 was not simply a historical milestone; it was the literal fulfillment of one of the most vivid prophecies in the Bible. For nearly two thousand years, the Jewish people were scattered across the world—persecuted, expelled, and seemingly erased as a unified people. And yet, through divine orchestration, they returned to their ancestral homeland and reestablished a sovereign state in the land of their forefathers.

The prophet Ezekiel was shown a vision in which he was led by the Spirit of the Lord to a valley full of dry bones:

> Then he said to me, "Son of man, these bones are the whole house of Israel. They say, 'Our bones are dried up and our hope is gone; we are cut off.' Therefore prophesy and say to them: 'This is what the Sovereign Lord says: My people, I am going to open your graves and bring you up from them; I will bring you back to the land of Israel'" (Ezek 37:11–12).

This prophecy, delivered over twenty-five hundred years ago, could hardly be more accurate. After centuries of exile, pogroms, the Holocaust, and wandering, the rebirth of Israel happened almost overnight. On May 14, 1948, David Ben-Gurion declared

Israel's independence, and within hours the new state was under military attack from surrounding Muslim nations. This immediate hostility highlights the spiritual resistance to God's prophetic fulfillment.

It is acknowledged in the Qur'an that the land was given to the Jews: "And We said thereafter to the Children of Israel, 'Dwell securely in the land (of promise)'" (Q 17:104). Yet Islamic ideology has shifted over time, claiming the land belongs solely to Muslims, leading to an ongoing contradiction.

Islamic nations contest the legitimacy of Israel's existence, often invoking the term *occupation* to describe Jewish presence in Jerusalem, despite both scriptural and historical claims. The very bones that were once scattered have now risen—and the world, both spiritual and political, has taken notice.

The conflict over Israel is not just about borders—it's about belief. The return of the Jews to Israel is a testament to the faithfulness of God. Yet instead of seeing it as proof of prophecy fulfilled, many respond with hostility, envy, or denial.

Jesus, foreseeing Jerusalem's future, warned, "They will fall by the sword and will be taken as prisoners to all the nations. Jerusalem will be trampled on by the Gentiles until the times of the Gentiles are fulfilled" (Luke 21:24). That time is being fulfilled in our generation.

The valley of dry bones is no longer lifeless. The body of Israel has returned. But the Spirit is still missing. As Ezekiel continues, "I will put my Spirit in you and you will live. . . . Then you will know that I the Lord have spoken, and I have done it, declares the Lord" (Ezek 37:14).

The restoration is physical first, but the spiritual awakening is coming. Just as God brought Israel back to life once, he will breathe into them again. And when they recognize the One they have pierced (Zech 12:10), the final chapter of redemption will begin.

Israel's return is not the end—it is the beginning of the countdown. The stage is set. The bones have risen. The Messiah is near.

11

The Temple Mount
A Ground Zero of Faith and Fury

AT THE VERY HEART of Jerusalem lies the Temple Mount—a single elevated platform of stone, yet perhaps the most spiritually and politically charged piece of real estate on earth. It is revered by Jews as the site of the First and Second Temples, by Christians as a location central to Jesus's ministry and prophecy, and by Muslims as the location of Al-Aqsa Mosque and the Dome of the Rock.

The Temple Mount is where Abraham was said to have prepared to sacrifice Isaac (Gen 22), where Solomon built the First Temple (1 Kgs 6), and where Zerubbabel, and later Herod, constructed the Second Temple (Ezra 6, John 2:20). For Jews, it is the holiest site in the world. And yet, for nearly two thousand years, Jews have been unable to worship there freely.

Muslims believe that Muhammad ascended to heaven from this location during the Isra and Mi'raj—a claim that was established centuries after his death and is referenced indirectly in Q 17:1. The construction of the Dome of the Rock in 691 CE and the Al-Aqsa Mosque shortly after cemented Islamic claims over the site. Since then, it has remained under Muslim control, with Jordan's waqf administering it to this day.

The Temple Mount

This overlap is no coincidence—it is the fault line of a much deeper spiritual conflict. For Jews, the Third Temple must be built on this site for the Messiah to come. For Muslims, any such construction is seen as a desecration and an existential threat.

Jesus himself made a prophetic and controversial statement about the temple: "Destroy this temple, and I will raise it again in three days" (John 2:19). He was speaking of his body, indicating that the physical temple was merely a shadow of the true dwelling place of God. But more than that, his resurrection after three days became the foundation upon which the church was built—the spiritual temple of believers. As Eph 2:20-21 explains, the church is "built on the foundation of the apostles and prophets, with Christ Jesus himself as the chief cornerstone." His claim was not metaphorical alone; it became historical reality, as the global church—alive across every continent—is living proof of his divinity and resurrection power (John 2:19).

Yet, he also prophesied its destruction (Matt 24:2), which came to pass in 70 CE when Roman forces under Titus obliterated the Second Temple and much of Jerusalem.

Since then, Christians believe the true temple is found in Christ himself and within the body of believers: "Don't you know that you yourselves are God's temple and that God's Spirit dwells in your midst?" (1 Cor 3:16).

The irony is striking. The very site meant to be a house of prayer for all nations (Isa 56:7) has become a place of exclusion, surveillance, and tension. Jewish pilgrims are restricted, Christian groups are often met with hostility, and any talk of rebuilding ignites international outrage.

In Islamic eschatology, Jerusalem is seen as the eventual center of Islamic rule in the end times. In Jewish prophecy, it is the city from which the Messiah will reign. And in Christian belief, it is where Christ will return and establish his kingdom. All three faiths point to this one place—but only one truth can prevail.

The Temple Mount is not just a sacred site; it is a mirror of humanity's spiritual struggle. Control of it reflects not just military or political dominance, but a claim to spiritual authority. And as long as the mount is contested, peace will remain elusive. The fury surrounding it is not accidental—it is the tremor before a divine earthquake.

As Ps 132:13–14 declares, "For the Lord has chosen Zion, he has desired it for his dwelling, saying, 'This is my resting place forever and ever; here I will sit enthroned, for I have desired it.'"

The Temple Mount is not just contested ground. It is God's chosen hill—and history will culminate there.

12

Messiah vs. Mahdi

The Battle for Divine Authority

THIS RAISES A VITAL question: If Jesus's divinity had already been known, accepted, and worshipped across many parts of the world for over six hundred years, why would God suddenly correct this belief through a solitary man in a cave with no direct witnesses or corroboration?

If Christians were wrong to believe Jesus is the Son of God—based on eyewitness testimony, miracles, fulfilled prophecies, and centuries of transformative faith—what, precisely, was the mistake? Where is the historical or theological failure so severe that God would need to send an angel with a contradictory message, effectively rewriting the entire redemptive narrative that the apostles died to proclaim?

Islam's claim that Jesus is not divine, nor the Son of God, comes not during the time of the apostles, nor even during the first centuries when doctrinal debates were still forming—but only after Christianity had firmly shaped the spiritual and moral foundation of the known world. The Christian message had spread from Israel to Rome, from Africa to Asia Minor, transforming societies, elevating the dignity of individuals, building hospitals, universities, and cathedrals. The modern Common Era (CE) is based not on the life of Muhammad, but on the life of Christ. The very calendar by which the world operates acknowledges his centrality.

So why contradict it? If Jesus is not who Christians believe he is, then Islam must demonstrate not only why it's right—but why Christianity's spiritual fruit, miraculous accounts, and moral revolution are wrong.

Instead, what we see are countless examples—documented miracles at Christian sites, incorruptible saints, visions, healings, and ongoing testimonies—that affirm the presence of divine truth in the belief that Jesus is Lord. No similar legacy exists with comparable global impact in Islamic history. Islam has produced empires, laws, and sciences—but it has not produced the same universal transformation of heart and soul centered on divine love and sacrificial grace.

To say that Christians have made a mistake is to ignore the entire legacy of the gospel—its evidence, its impact, and its prophetic fulfillment. And if no mistake is evident, the contradiction introduced by Islam appears not as correction from God, but as disruption from another source.

The logic does not hold: that after six hundred years of gospel witness, God suddenly declares his own Son is not his Son, and that the entire redemptive plan was misinterpreted. If Allah is, as described in the Qur'an, "the best of planners" (Q 8:30), then why would he allow centuries of believers to follow what Islam claims is a mistake? Would the best planner let millions believe in the divinity of Jesus—confirming his virgin birth, miracles, and sinlessness—only to later contradict it with a message that undermines his entire identity?

This raises a troubling inconsistency. If Jesus was merely a prophet like Muhammad, wouldn't the best of planners have made that clear from the beginning, preventing such a foundational "error"? Instead, Islam asserts that God's message had to be corrected six centuries later, through a single man with no eyewitnesses, manuscripts, or links to the Hebrew or Christian Scriptures. That is not divine foresight—that is contradiction.

The logic, again, collapses. One cannot call Allah the best planner and simultaneously argue that the belief in Jesus as divine was a mistake so widespread it required rewriting divine history. True divine planning does not require correction—it fulfills prophecy with clarity and purpose, as Jesus did. If God is not a God of confusion (1 Cor 14:33), why would he bring contradiction rather than clarity?

LOGIC CHECK: THE BEST PLANNER?

If Allah is truly "the best of planners" (Q 8:30), then:

- Why allow belief in Jesus's divinity to spread globally for six hundred years?
- Why confirm his virgin birth, miracles, and sinlessness, yet deny his crucifixion and resurrection?
- Why correct his identity through a single man, with no eyewitnesses, centuries later?

A perfect plan doesn't require revision. Truth doesn't require contradiction. If Jesus was merely a prophet, this would have been made clear at the beginning—not after the gospel had transformed the world.

And the center of that truth is Jesus Christ.

13

The Last Temple and the Return of the King

IN THE YEAR 70 CE, the Roman general Titus led the siege of Jerusalem and destroyed the Second Temple, fulfilling Jesus's prophecy in Matt 24:2: "Not one stone here will be left on another; every one will be thrown down." This event marked the end of the sacrificial system and temple-based worship in Judaism. For Christians, however, it signified the completion of a transition—from the physical temple to the spiritual presence of God through Christ.

Not long after this, as Christianity spread across the Roman Empire, Emperor Constantine's mother, Helena, traveled to the Holy Land around 326 CE. According to tradition, she identified the site believed to be Golgotha—the place of Jesus's crucifixion—and his nearby tomb. In response, Constantine ordered the construction of the Church of the Holy Sepulchre, which still stands today. Built on the very spot where Jesus is believed to have been buried and resurrected, the church became the spiritual center of Christianity, replacing the Temple Mount as the focal point of divine encounter.

The Last Temple and the Return of the King

While the temple was once the earthly meeting place between God and man, Jesus's resurrection redirected the world's attention from a building to a person. The presence of God no longer dwelt in a temple made of stone, but in the risen Christ. The Church of the Holy Sepulchre thus became a living monument to the new covenant—a physical testimony that Jesus had fulfilled what the temple symbolized.

This transformation was not just theological, but geopolitical. As Judaism mourned the loss of its temple and Muslims later vied to claim the Temple Mount for their own, Christianity rooted its identity not in conquest or land, but in the person of Christ and the miracle of the empty tomb.

From Genesis to Revelation, the temple has always been more than a building. It is the meeting place between God and man—a place where heaven touches earth. The destruction of the First Temple by the Babylonians, and the Second by the Romans, were not only historical tragedies for the Jewish people, but spiritual signs pointing to something deeper: the end of one era, and the foreshadowing of another.

Yet, biblical prophecy tells us a Third Temple must arise. According to Dan 9:27, the antichrist will "confirm a covenant with many for one 'seven,' but in the middle of the 'seven' he will put an end to sacrifice and offering." This assumes a rebuilt temple with active sacrifices—a direct challenge to the once-for-all sacrifice made by Jesus (Heb 10:10). Revelation 11:1–2 also speaks of the temple being measured, and of the gentiles trampling the holy city for forty-two months.

So, what is this final temple? Is it physical? Is it symbolic? Is it both?

Christians believe Jesus himself became the temple: "Destroy this temple, and I will raise it again in three days" (John 2:19). He was referring to his body—showing that the true dwelling of God is no longer in stone and wood, but in Christ and in his followers: "Do you not know that your bodies are temples of the Holy Spirit?" (1 Cor 6:19).

However, the Jewish people still await a physical restoration—and for many, the rebuilding of the temple is a prerequisite for the coming of the Messiah. Ironically, the very One they wait for has already come—and was rejected. Thus, the rebuilding of the Third Temple, if pursued without faith in Christ, may unwittingly prepare the world not for the return of the true King, but for the rise of the counterfeit one.

Muslims, too, have a stake in this site—the Dome of the Rock, built on the Temple Mount, sits directly where the Jewish holy of holies once stood. Islamic tradition claims the prophet Muhammad ascended to heaven from this site during the Isra and Mi'raj. Thus, the claim to Jerusalem becomes not just territorial but eschatological.

In this spiritual clash, the final temple will become the ultimate battleground—not just of armies, but of truth. The antichrist, Scripture tells us, will "set himself up in God's temple, proclaiming himself to be God" (2 Thess 2:4). This is the final deception, when the false messiah will seek to take the throne—not by spirit, but by force.

But just as darkness reaches its peak, the sky will split. The King will return—not as a suffering servant, but as a conquering warrior: "They will look on me, the one they have pierced" (Zech 12:10). And when he sets his feet on the Mount of Olives (Zech 14:4), the true temple will be restored—not built by human hands, but revealed in glory.

The final temple is Christ. The final kingdom is his. And the final victory belongs to the Lamb.

14

Signs in the East

Persia, Prophecy, and the Powers Behind the Curtain

WHILE ISRAEL OFTEN SITS at the center of the world's attention, it is impossible to understand the full scope of the conflict without examining the forces brewing in the East—particularly in Persia, now known as Iran. Historically a cradle of empires and philosophy, Persia has today become a geopolitical and theological antagonist to Israel and the West, with deep spiritual undertones that go beyond nuclear tensions and military alliances.

In the Bible, Persia appears repeatedly:

- In Dan 10:13, an angel speaks of being resisted by the "Prince of Persia," a clear reference not just to a human ruler but to a territorial spiritual power.

- Esther's story unfolds in Persia, where God's providence preserved the Jewish people from genocide.

- Cyrus the Great, a Persian king, is even called God's "anointed" (Isa 45:1) for allowing the Jews to return and rebuild Jerusalem.

But the modern regime in Iran seeks the opposite: the destruction of Israel. They openly declare their intent to wipe Israel off the map. What drives such intense hatred? Is it merely politics, or is there an ancient enmity resurfacing?

Iran's leadership, rooted in Shia Islam, believes in the coming of the Mahdi—the Twelfth Imam, a messianic figure who will return to establish Islamic justice. Crucially, they believe that chaos and war are necessary to hasten his return. This belief system stands in direct opposition to the gospel, where peace is not forced through conflict but offered through Christ's sacrificial love.

Iran's interest in Jerusalem isn't just symbolic. Many analysts have noted that Iran desires to relocate the center of Islamic authority from Mecca to Jerusalem—removing Saudi Arabia's theological control and fulfilling a long-term goal of religious supremacy. To do this, the Temple Mount must fall under Islamic authority, and any Jewish rebuilding effort must be stopped.

We are not simply witnessing a clash of civilizations. We are seeing a collision of destinies—one that stretches back to the garden of Eden, was prophesied in Daniel and Revelation, and will culminate with the return of Christ. The powers at play are not only governments but spiritual principalities (Eph 6:12).

Just as God raised Cyrus to liberate Israel, so, too, he raises and removes rulers to fulfill his plans. Iran's current aggression, while terrifying, fits within the permitted boundaries of divine sovereignty. Evil is allowed—but never in control. Every empire that has risen against God's people has eventually fallen. Babylon. Rome. And one day, modern Persia.

Jesus said in Matt 24:6–7, "You will hear of wars and rumors of wars. . . . Nation will rise against nation, and kingdom against kingdom." Yet he included this: "See that you are not alarmed. Such things must happen."

This is not the end. But it is a sign. A sign that the curtain is lifting, and the final act is nearing. And as always, God remains the author of history—writing the victory in advance.

Moreover, it's vital to understand that global politics are playing directly into the script foretold in the Bible. Whether knowingly or not, world leaders are entangled in the prophetic narrative—making decisions that align with the ancient story centered on Israel. If you, the reader, think you are disconnected from these plans, remember this: your nation's leaders have already been involved—and will continue to be involved—in the conflict surrounding Israel until the end of the age. This is not just Israel's war. It is humanity's.

Nations involved directly or indirectly include: the United States, Russia, Iran, Turkey, Syria, Egypt, Saudi Arabia, Lebanon, Jordan, China, France, the United Kingdom, Germany, and others through alliances such as NATO and the United Nations.

Ignorance of this reality does not insulate one from its consequences. Pretending it is irrelevant does not stop its unfolding.

SCRIPTURE ECHO—PERSIA AND THE END TIMES

- Daniel 10:13—"The prince of the Persian kingdom resisted me twenty-one days." (Spiritual warfare behind empires)
- Isaiah 45:1—"This is what the Lord says to his anointed, to Cyrus . . ." (God uses Persia for his plan)
- Revelation 16:12—"The sixth angel poured out his bowl on the great river Euphrates . . ." (Geographical preparation for Armageddon)
- Ephesians 6:12—"For we wrestle not against flesh and blood, but against . . . the powers of this dark world."

These verses remind us: what unfolds in politics often reflects what is happening in the heavens.

15

The False Singularity
When Unity Becomes a Lie

IN TODAY'S RAPIDLY EVOLVING world, we hear increasing calls for unity, global consciousness, and collective harmony. From the halls of the United Nations to Silicon Valley tech summits, the idea is repeated endlessly: humanity must become "one" in order to survive. On the surface, this sounds noble. But beneath this seemingly virtuous message lies a profound deception—what we will call the false singularity.

A singularity, in scientific terms, refers to a point where known laws collapse—like the center of a black hole, or the theorized moment of creation. In artificial intelligence and philosophy, "the singularity" has come to represent a tipping point—when AI surpasses human intelligence, or when humanity transcends biology and merges with machine. But in spiritual terms, this concept mirrors something far older: the desire to become like God without God.

This idea is not new. In Gen 3:5, the serpent promised Eve, "You will be like God." That was the first singularity. It was a rebellion against the created order. Today, we see this rebellion revived through global movements that seek oneness without the cross, morality without the Messiah, and peace without truth.

The False Singularity

From New Age spirituality to transhumanism, from interfaith councils to universalist theology, the cry is the same: Let us all be one—but without Jesus.

But what does true unity look like?

Jesus said, "I and the Father are one" (John 10:30), and again, "That they may all be one, just as you, Father, are in me and I in you" (John 17:21). The gospel offers the real singularity—unity not through technology or political agreement, but through rebirth in Christ. Any other form of unity is counterfeit.

As we move closer to the end, the world will increasingly seek a false savior—one who promises to unite all people, religions, and ideologies under a banner of tolerance and progress. But this is the very image Revelation warns about—a beast that speaks peace but leads to worship of the dragon (Rev 13:4-8).

Today's globalist movements speak of love, progress, and shared humanity, but systematically erase the distinct truth of Jesus Christ. That is not unity. That is uniformity imposed by deception.

WARNING SIGNS OF THE FALSE SINGULARITY

- Religious syncretism—claiming all faiths are equal paths to God.
- AI and spiritual consciousness merging—replacing the soul with circuitry.
- Global governance—where values are decided by human consensus, not divine authority.
- Moral relativism—where truth becomes subjective and sin is redefined.

This modern "Babel" is reaching toward heaven once again—not with bricks and mortar, but with code and ideology. And just as God scattered the people in Gen 11, so, too, will he bring down every tower built in rebellion against him.

The true singularity is not a moment in time. It is a person—Jesus Christ, the One through whom all things were made, and in whom all things hold together (Col 1:16–17). He alone unites heaven and earth. He alone reconciles God and man.

TRUTH VS. LIE—DISCERNING THE REAL FROM THE IMITATION

One

> Truth: "I am the way, the truth, and the life. No one comes to the Father except through me."—Jesus (John 14:6)
>
> Example: Christianity declares that salvation is found only through Jesus Christ, based on eyewitness testimony, fulfilled prophecy, and a bodily resurrection.
>
> Lie: "All religions lead to the same God."
>
> Example: The modern interfaith movement pushes the idea that Islam, Buddhism, Hinduism, and Christianity all hold equal truth—yet they fundamentally contradict one another on who God is, what sin is, and how salvation works.

Two

> Truth: God is the Creator who made man in his image.
>
> Example: Gen 1:27 affirms humans are sacred, created with inherent dignity and eternal purpose.
>
> Lie: Humanity is evolving into gods through technology and consciousness.
>
> Example: Transhumanist goals of merging AI with human biology aim to "upgrade" mankind, implying divine evolution without God.

Three

Truth: Jesus is the Light of the world, and no darkness can overcome him (John 8:12).

Example: The gospel calls people to repentance, humility, and faith in Jesus as the only way to eternal life.

Lie: Enlightenment is found through inner energy, meditation, or mystical experience.

Example: New Age practices suggest divinity can be unlocked through self-awareness, yoga, or spirit guides—bypassing the need for a savior.

Four

Truth: True unity comes through the Holy Spirit, who dwells in all believers.

Example: In Acts 2, people of different nations and tongues were united in Christ by the Spirit, not by ideology or force.

Lie: Peace comes from government regulation and shared values.

Example: Globalist agendas promote peace through international law, social conformity, and surveillance—often silencing dissenters in the name of unity.

Five

Truth: God is sovereign, and history unfolds according to his will.

Example: Biblical prophecy has repeatedly shown accuracy in geopolitical events (e.g., fall of Babylon, rebirth of Israel).

Lie: The future is in humanity's hands—we must save the planet and evolve morally.

Example: Climate politics and UN speeches often carry messianic tones, calling people to "save the earth" while ignoring the Creator.

Six

Truth: Jesus is returning physically to judge the nations and reign forever.

Example: Rev 19 describes Christ on a white horse, bringing justice and defeating evil once and for all.

Lie: A "messianic" world leader will solve all our problems.

Example: As global instability rises, people look for charismatic leaders who promise peace, economic stability, and religious tolerance—foreshadowing the rise of the antichrist.

These contrasts reveal the deeper battle: not between West and East, but between truth and deception, Christ and antichrist, Creator and counterfeiter.

When truth is denied, a lie doesn't vanish—it replaces the truth. And the cost of believing that lie will be eternal.

16

The Spirit and the Bride Say, "Come"

The Role of the Church Before the End

AMID THE THUNDER OF war, deception, and rising darkness, there remains a quiet yet unstoppable force in the world—the church. Though often persecuted, ridiculed, or politically sidelined, the church is not just a passive observer in this conflict. It is God's living body on earth, tasked with both preserving truth and inviting the lost into salvation before the final curtain falls.

Jesus said, "You are the light of the world. A city set on a hill cannot be hidden" (Matt 5:14). In the context of growing global delusion—where the true gospel is being diluted, ignored, or reinterpreted—the remnant church is more vital than ever.

THE ORIGINS OF THE CHURCH—FROM PENTECOST TO GLOBAL MISSION

The church began at Pentecost, when the Holy Spirit descended on the disciples in Jerusalem (Acts 2). From that moment, the message of Christ spread across the Roman Empire, through persecution, martyrdom, and miracles. The early church transformed history, not by conquest, but by love, truth, and sacrifice.

It was Christians who:

- Cared for the sick and poor in times of plague when others fled.
- Rescued abandoned infants from Roman trash heaps.
- Preserved and copied ancient texts, saving Western civilization during the Dark Ages.
- Laid the foundations for modern science, education, and law.
- Built hospitals, orphanages, and schools in every continent.

The first church building identified by archaeology is the Dura-Europos house church in Syria, dated to around 233 CE. But the church existed in homes and underground gatherings long before that—because its true strength was never in bricks, but in boldness.

Even the discovery of the Americas was guided by a vision tied to Christianity. Columbus recorded in his journal that he believed God gave him the purpose to bring the Gospel to unknown lands.

The moral frameworks of justice, mercy, and human dignity are all deeply rooted in Christian theology. Without the church, there would be no Magna Carta, no abolition of slavery, no civil rights movement as we know it.

HOW THE CHURCH CHANGED CIVILIZATION

Slavery Abolished by Christian Influence

William Wilberforce, a devout Christian, led the charge to abolish the transatlantic slave trade in the British Empire. His Christian conviction drove decades of political struggle that ended with the Slave Trade Act of 1807 and Slavery Abolition Act of 1833.

In America, many abolitionists were pastors and believers, including Harriet Beecher Stowe (author of *Uncle Tom's Cabin*) and Frederick Douglass, who preached the incompatibility of slavery with the gospel.

Civil Rights Rooted in Christian Justice

Dr. Martin Luther King Jr. was a Baptist minister who quoted Scripture constantly. His dream was not rooted in political rebellion, but in biblical justice: "Let justice roll on like a river, righteousness like a never-failing stream" (Amos 5:24).

The Civil Rights Movement's most powerful marches began in churches, with prayer and hymn-singing. It was faith in Christ that empowered nonviolence in the face of hate.

Penal and Civil Codes Shaped by Biblical Law

Many modern legal systems are based on biblical law—particularly the Ten Commandments. The ideas of witness testimony, perjury, justice for the poor, and restitution all flow from Scripture.

In Western tradition, the idea of innocent until proven guilty and due process trace back to Judeo-Christian values.

The phrase "Do the right thing" reflects Jesus's teachings—especially Matt 25, where he says he will separate people as a shepherd separates sheep from goats, with the righteous going to his right hand.

Language and Morality

Common phrases like "Turn the other cheek," "Go the extra mile," or "Let him who is without sin cast the first stone" all come from Jesus.

The very idea that all people are created equal comes not from Greek philosophy but from Gen 1:27—"So God created mankind in his own image."

Today, people take for granted the progress achieved—yet they forget who helped build the bridge. They enjoy the fruits of the gospel while scorning the tree that bore them.

THE CHURCH'S MISSION BEFORE THE END

1. To bear witness to the truth
   The church proclaims that Jesus is Lord, crucified and risen, the only way to salvation. In a time when truth is considered subjective and religious pluralism dominates, this message is offensive—and necessary.

   > This gospel of the kingdom will be preached in the whole world . . . and then the end will come. (Matt 24:14)

2. To call the world to repentance
   The church is not called to blend into the culture but to call it out of its rebellion. Just like the prophets before her, the church must cry, "Repent, for the kingdom of heaven is near!" (Matt 3:2).

   > Come out of her, my people, so that you will not share in her sins. (Rev 18:4)

3. The be the bride—waiting, longing, preparing
   The church is not only a preacher—it is also a bride. A bride adorned for her husband, waiting for the return of her King. Revelation 22:17 says, "The Spirit and the Bride say, 'Come.'" This is both a prayer and a declaration:
   Come, Lord Jesus—end this conflict.
   Come, lost soul—find grace before it's too late.
   This cry is not made out of fear but out of love. We long for his appearing, not to escape suffering, but to see the King of kings take his rightful place.

4. To be a church at war—not with weapons, but with truth
   Ephesians 6 reminds us that our battle is not with flesh and blood but with principalities, powers, and rulers of darkness.

The Spirit and the Bride Say, "Come"

As the world arms itself with nuclear weapons, artificial intelligence, and surveillance, the church arms herself with:

- The word of God—sharper than any sword.
- The gospel of peace—which transforms hearts, not just policies.
- The name of Jesus—against which no demon can stand.

The apostate church will rise as a counterfeit to the bride. The Bible warns that not all who claim Christ are truly his. In Revelation, a false woman also appears—the great prostitute, Babylon, dressed in splendor but filled with corruption:

> She held a golden cup . . . filled with abominable things and the filth of her adulteries. (Rev 17:4)

This counterfeit church promotes unity at the cost of truth. It preaches tolerance but denies repentance. It accepts all gods but rejects the Son. It will be embraced by the world—and judged by God.

The global church today is persecuted but powerful. In Iran, underground churches grow. In China, Christians meet in secret. In Africa and Latin America, revival spreads. And even in the secular West, a remnant remains—small, perhaps, but burning with truth:

> The gates of hell shall not prevail against it. (Matt 16:18)

There will be a final call before the return of Jesus, when the world will see two types of churches:

- One that reflects Christ, filled with the Spirit.
- One that reflects the world, filled with compromise.

You must decide which voice you will follow:

- The Spirit and the true bride will say, "Come."
- The false church will say, "Stay and prosper."

Truth, Peace, and Faith

In a world flooded with competing truths, glowing screens, and global narratives, it's easy to be swept into the current of collective thinking. But the gospel calls us not to conformity—it calls us to truth, no matter how unpopular or costly. The real singularity has already come: God entered history as Jesus Christ. The cross is the axis on which eternity turns.

You, reader, are not just an observer in this unfolding conflict. You are part of it. The greatest deception is not believing a lie—it's thinking the truth doesn't matter. But it does. Eternity depends on it.

Will you follow the true Light, or the brightest imitation?

> Lord Jesus,
> In a world of confusion and imitation, open my eyes to your truth.
> Guard my heart from false unity and counterfeit peace.
> Help me see through the lies that sound sweet but lead to death.
> Make me bold to stand for you, even when the world pushes me to conform.
> You are the way, the truth, and the life—let me follow no one else.
> Unite my heart with yours, and let me walk in the real singularity:
> You.
> Amen.

17

The Nations Rage
Global Politics and the Prophecies of God

AS THE WORLD SPINS ever faster into division, rebellion, and moral confusion, many remain unaware that the very political forces shaping modern history were foretold in Scripture. From ancient empires to current superpowers, the hand of prophecy has been guiding and warning humanity all along. Yet many still believe they are outside of God's plan—untouched by the battle unfolding in the Middle East.

But the reality is this: every nation is involved, whether directly or indirectly, and no leader can escape the gravity of what is to come.

> Why do the nations rage and the peoples plot in vain?
> The kings of the earth rise up and the rulers band together against the Lord and against his Anointed. (Ps 2:1–2)

A WORLD DRAWN INTO THE CONFLICT

The modern State of Israel was reestablished in 1948. Since then, nearly every nation on earth has had to form a position on Israel—politically, militarily, economically, or spiritually.

The United States supports Israel financially and militarily—but even that support has fluctuated under different administrations.

Russia has aligned itself with Syria and Iran—both enemies of Israel—echoing the Ezek 38 prophecy where Gog of Magog leads a northern coalition against the land of Israel.

China, while historically silent, now seeks influence in the region as part of its global expansion—economically through the Belt and Road Initiative, and geopolitically through the UN.

The European Union struggles with internal division over Israeli policy, often prioritizing diplomacy and energy deals over biblical truth.

Muslim nations like Iran, Lebanon (via Hezbollah), and Yemen (via the Houthis) have declared intentions to wipe Israel from the map.

Even South American and African nations, though far removed, take sides in global forums like the UN General Assembly.

No one is neutral. Just as Revelation describes a final gathering of nations around Israel (Rev 16:14–16), so, too, we are seeing the slow formation of alliances and rivalries that match biblical prophecy.

SCRIPTURE AND THE SHAPE OF GLOBAL POLICY

God declared that Israel would be "a cup of trembling" and "a burdensome stone for all nations" (Zech 12:2–3). This prophecy makes little sense unless you understand the spiritual significance of Israel, Jerusalem, and the Temple Mount.

Modern secularism claims to operate above religious belief. Yet the most enduring and volatile political debates remain religious at their core—the land, the temple, the Messiah.

Even legal and philosophical frameworks around justice, law, and morality were influenced by biblical principles:

- The US Declaration of Independence: "All men are created equal" echoes Gen 1:27.

- The Geneva Conventions, defining the ethics of war, were rooted in Christian principles of just war and human dignity.
- Human rights charters around the world adopt language like "inalienable rights"—a term created by Christian thinkers to describe what God has given that man cannot revoke.
- Penal codes against murder, theft, false witness, and perjury mirror the Ten Commandments (Exod 20).
- Even civil codes, including property rights and contractual law, carry echoes of Mosaic law found in Leviticus and Deuteronomy.

The global political and moral language we use today, such as "Do the right thing," finds origin in Christian ethics. The idea of right and wrong was transformed by Jesus, who taught that the sheep will be placed on the right side of the Father (Matt 25:33)—meaning righteousness and approval.

TIMELINE OF PROPHETIC FULFILLMENT IN POLITICS

- 70 CE—Romans destroy the Second Temple, scattering the Jews.
- 313 CE—Christianity legalized in the Roman Empire under Constantine.
- 1099 CE—First Crusade captures Jerusalem from Muslim control.
- 1517 CE—Protestant Reformation challenges the apostate church.
- 1917 CE—Balfour Declaration expresses British support for a Jewish homeland.
- 1948 CE—Modern State of Israel is born—a direct fulfillment of Ezek 36–37.

- 1967 CE—Israel recaptures Jerusalem in the Six-Day War, aligning with Luke 21:24.
- Present Day—Nations gather in coalitions, forming the groundwork of Gog of Magog (Ezek 38), and the kings of the East (Rev 16:12).

GLOBAL INDIFFERENCE IS NOT NEUTRALITY

Many modern people believe that by "not getting involved" they are neutral. But ignoring God's plan doesn't remove you from it. It places you outside of his protection and on the wrong side of history.

> He who is not with me is against me. (Matt 12:30)

Whether one supports or opposes Israel, or simply avoids the conversation entirely, every nation—and every individual—is part of the unfolding drama between God and Lucifer, between truth and deception, between Christ and antichrist.

YOUR NATION IS NOT EXEMPT

Reader, if you believe that your country or your leaders are separate from these events, understand this: the policies your leaders make regarding Israel, truth, and the church will determine blessing or judgment.

> I will bless those who bless you, and whoever curses you
> I will curse. (Gen 12:3)

Today, world governments speak in terms of peace agreements, ceasefires, and diplomatic resolutions. But the root issue is spiritual, and the outcome is already foretold. The true King is returning to claim his throne.

YOU ARE IN THE PROPHECY

Reader, you are not exempt. Your passport may not say "Israel," but your soul belongs to a greater kingdom. Either you belong to the Lamb who was slain, or to the world system that opposes him.

The nations rage—but they rage against Christ. And he will return to silence them.

> The kingdoms of this world have become the kingdom of our Lord and of his Christ, and he shall reign forever and ever. (Rev 11:15)

FINAL REFLECTION

If you believe politics and prophecy are unrelated, consider this: your nation's very existence, values, freedoms, and laws have already been shaped by biblical ideas—and will soon be tested by them. The conflict in Israel is not "someone else's war." It is a mirror of the war in your heart.

You must choose a side.

And there is only one King who will rule them all.

18

The Final War
Truth vs. Deception

EVERY AGE HAS HAD its conflicts. But the final war, unlike any before it, is not merely about land, religion, or power. It is a war for the very essence of truth—a global confrontation between what God has revealed and what Satan has twisted.

> Woe to those who call evil good and good evil, who put darkness for light and light for darkness. (Isa 5:20)

This is not a conventional war. It is a war of ideas, symbols, loyalties, and eternal destinies. It's not fought only with weapons, but with words, policies, media, education, and spiritual influence. It is everywhere—in the streets, in schools, in parliaments, and even in pulpits.

THE WEAPON OF DECEPTION

From the very beginning, Lucifer's most powerful weapon was deception. In the garden of Eden, he did not force Adam and Eve—he convinced them. He lied—subtly. And it worked.

Today, Satan uses the same methods:

- Redefine truth: "What's true for you isn't true for me."
- Blur the lines: "All religions are the same."
- Distract the soul: "Just live your truth. Be happy. That's what matters."
- Ridicule the gospel: "You still believe in that ancient book?"

And so, even those with Bibles in their homes are deceived. They have heard of Jesus but never met him. They follow a culturally approved Christianity—one that tolerates all but transforms nothing.

THE POWER OF TRUTH

Jesus said, "You will know the truth, and the truth will set you free" (John 8:32). This final war is not just about resisting evil—it's about clinging to truth with all your heart, even when the world calls it hate.

> Sanctify them by the truth; Your word is truth. (John 17:17)

Truth is not just a concept. Truth is a person—Jesus Christ. And he said, "I am the way, the truth, and the life. No one comes to the Father except through me." (John 14:6)

That's why this war is so intense. The devil knows the truth saves—and he will do anything to distract, distort, or destroy it before people find it.

TRUTH VS. LIE—IN CONTRAST

The gospel declares that Jesus is the Son of God, the Word made flesh (John 1:1–14). Islam, however, teaches in Q 4:171 that Jesus is no more than a messenger. Yet this contradicts their own text in Q 3:49, where Jesus gives life to a clay bird—a miracle no other prophet performs, and a divine act reserved for God.

Jesus taught to love your enemies and bless those who persecute you (Matt 5:44). This is a radical contrast to jihadist ideologies that encourage the destruction of enemies in the name of God.

The Bible teaches that all human life is sacred, made in the image of God (Gen 1:27). Yet in the world today, life is often treated as a personal choice, and the sanctity of life is replaced by convenience.

Scripture teaches that salvation is a gift of grace (Eph 2:8–9), not by works. In contrast, many religious systems—including legalistic forms of Christianity and Islam—promote salvation through deeds and performance, which denies the sufficiency of the cross.

The Bible clearly states that God created male and female (Gen 1:27). Today's cultural ideologies claim gender is fluid—a social construct. This confusion is not evolution but rebellion.

Proverbs 9:10 declares that "the fear of the Lord is the beginning of wisdom." Yet modern education removes God entirely, replacing reverence with relativism.

These are not mere philosophical disagreements—they are eternal collisions between what God has spoken and what Satan wants us to believe.

THE BATTLE IN THE MIND AND SPIRIT

The battlefield is not only in Jerusalem or political capitals. It is in every human heart.

> The god of this age has blinded the minds of unbelievers.
> (2 Cor 4:4)

Satan has no real power over a Christian—but he can cloud vision, distort truth, and sow confusion if we are not rooted in the word.

The Armor of God

Paul writes in Eph 6:11-17 that believers must wear spiritual armor:

- Belt of truth
- Breastplate of righteousness
- Shoes of the gospel of peace
- Shield of faith
- Helmet of salvation
- Sword of the Spirit—the word of God

This is how we fight. Not with anger or fear—but with truth, peace, and faith.

THE RISE OF THE ANTICHRIST SPIRIT

The world is being prepared for one final lie—that man can be God. Technology, AI, transhumanism, and "oneness" philosophies are paving the way for a false messiah. This antichrist will:

- Appear as a savior of mankind.
- Perform signs and wonders.
- Demand worship.
- Turn the world against those who follow Christ.

But his kingdom will fall.

> Then the lawless one will be revealed ... whom the Lord Jesus will overthrow with the breath of his mouth. (2 Thess 2:8)

THE FINAL CALL TO TRUTH

Dear reader, the war is not coming. It is already here. You must choose your side now. This is not a call to violence—it is a call to clarity.

> Choose this day whom you will serve. (Josh 24:15)

Truth is not a suggestion. It is a sword. And that sword is in your hands.

19

The Garden, the Serpent, and the Origins of Evil

ONE OF THE DEEPEST theological questions humanity has ever wrestled with is this: Why was Lucifer—the serpent—allowed into the garden of Eden in the first place? If Eden was paradise, why allow a being of deception and evil to enter at all?

The answer lies in the nature of love and free will. A world without choice is a world without genuine love. Adam and Eve were not created as robots but as image-bearers of God, endowed with the freedom to love, obey, and trust—or not.

Lucifer's presence in the garden was not a design flaw. It was a divine decision to allow freedom, and therefore the possibility of rebellion. Without the option to disobey, obedience is meaningless. Without the presence of evil, the pursuit of good lacks depth. God's perfect plan always included a test—not to make humanity fall, but to show what was truly in the human heart.

> You will not surely die. (Gen 3:4)

> When you eat of it your eyes will be opened, and you will be like God, knowing good and evil. (Gen 3:5)

Lucifer's temptation was a mirror of what he himself had wanted: to be like the Most High (Isa 14:14). By enticing Eve with the same desire, he tried to replicate his own fall within humanity.

But here is where God's genius outshines the enemy. Immediately after the fall, God declared the protoevangelium—the first Gospel:

> I will put enmity between you and the woman, and between your offspring and hers; he will crush your head, and you will strike his heel. (Gen 3:15)

This prophecy spoke of Jesus—the seed of the woman—who would one day be wounded by Satan (at the cross), but ultimately crush his power through resurrection.

The serpent's presence set the stage not only for humanity's fall but also for the redemption story that would follow. Without the fall, there would be no cross. Without the cross, there would be no demonstration of the depth of God's love, mercy, justice, and grace.

So why was Lucifer allowed into Eden?

Because freedom requires the possibility of temptation.

Because love cannot exist without choice.

Because God's plan was not to preserve innocence forever, but to grow his children into wisdom, righteousness, and maturity.

Lucifer's rebellion only revealed God's ultimate plan: to defeat evil not by brute force but by humility, sacrifice, and perfect righteousness.

In this light, Eden is not just the scene of humanity's fall. It is the launching point of God's eternal plan—a plan that will end with humanity not in a garden, but in a city, face to face with the Lamb who was slain.

> To the one who overcomes, I will give the right to eat from the tree of life, which is in the paradise of God. (Rev 2:7)

20

Divine Intelligence
Outsmarting Evil

WHAT IS INTELLIGENCE? FOR centuries, we've measured it in numbers: IQ scores, academic qualifications, problem-solving speed. But when we look at Scripture, we find an entirely different standard: true intelligence is the ability to recognize and overcome evil—to see God's truth and align with it.

There is no greater demonstration of this truth than in how God outsmarted Lucifer—not with violence, but with wisdom, humility, and a plan so profound that even Satan could not comprehend it.

THE CHECKMATE OF THE CROSS

From the beginning, Lucifer's goal was to thwart God's plan. When he encountered Jesus in the wilderness, he knew who he was:

> If you are the Son of God . . . (Matt 4:3, 6)

This wasn't a question—it was a challenge. Satan was fully aware that Jesus was divine. Yet, in his arrogance and spiritual blindness, he believed he could tempt God himself. Failing that, his backup plan was to kill Jesus, not realizing that by doing so, he would fulfill the very mission he sought to destroy.

> None of the rulers of this age understood it, for if they had, they would not have crucified the Lord of glory. (1 Cor 2:8)

The crucifixion was Satan's own defeat. He played right into God's hands. What he thought would be victory became his greatest loss.

This is divine intelligence—not the raw accumulation of knowledge, but the masterful unfolding of a plan that used evil's own weapons against itself.

REDEFINING INTELLIGENCE

In human systems, we reward intelligence that invents, calculates, memorizes, or builds. But in God's kingdom:

- Wisdom is greater than intellect.
- Obedience is greater than raw talent.
- Spiritual insight is greater than worldly cleverness.

Jesus said:

> Be wise as serpents and innocent as doves. (Matt 10:16)

He did not tell us to be merely educated or clever—but spiritually discerning, shrewd against the schemes of the enemy, and anchored in moral purity.

THE GRACE OF GOD IS THE HIGHEST INTELLIGENCE

Even more profound is this truth: intelligence is not something we achieve—it is something we receive. The Holy Spirit is the revealer of wisdom, insight, and discernment.

> The fear of the Lord is the beginning of wisdom. (Prov 9:10

When we surrender to God's grace, he opens our eyes. Suddenly, we see the traps of sin. We resist temptation. We walk away from lies. We step into light.

This is not worldly intelligence—it is eternal intelligence. It is the kind that defeats Satan.

A MESSAGE TO THE "UNQUALIFIED"

To those who were never top of the class, who never passed the exams, who were told they'd never amount to much—the world may have overlooked you, but God sees intelligence differently.

You are not judged by how much you know—but by what you do with the truth you've been given.

> God chose the foolish things of the world to shame the wise. (1 Cor 1:27)

Satan had unmatched knowledge—and yet he fell. Jesus, in his humility, triumphed through obedience. This is what we are called to imitate.

CONCLUSION: TRUE INTELLIGENCE IS MEASURED BY LIGHT

The smartest person in the world is not the one with the highest IQ—it's the one who can see through evil, who can discern God's voice, and who can choose truth when it costs something.

To outsmart the enemy is to align with Christ. That is the greatest intelligence of all.

21

The Tree of Life
Lost and Found

WHEN ADAM AND EVE disobeyed God and ate from the tree of the knowledge of good and evil, the consequences were immediate and profound. But hidden within the aftermath of that fall is a verse that raises an enormous question:

> He must not be allowed to reach out his hand and take also from the tree of life and eat, and live forever. (Gen 3:22)

Wait—what is the tree of life? Why was it in the garden? And why did God guard it with a flaming sword after the fall?

TWO TREES, TWO PATHS

In Eden, there were two significant trees:

1. The tree of the knowledge of good and evil—forbidden, the one that brought about the fall.
2. The tree of life—the one that gave immortality, now protected.

By eating from the first, humanity gained knowledge of good and evil—but in a fallen, sinful state. If they had then eaten from the tree of life, they would have lived forever in that corrupted condition. Out of mercy, God blocked their access.

> So the Lord God banished him from the garden . . . and placed a cherubim and a flaming sword . . . to guard the way to the tree of life. (Gen 3:23–24)

This was not punishment, but protection. God would not allow eternal life without redemption first.

THE LESSON HIDDEN IN THE TREES

The tree of knowledge taught us that there is no shortcut to understanding good and evil. We must experience the weight of suffering to truly grasp the value of good.

God didn't just punish—he allowed humanity to learn. To feel. To understand. It's as if God said: "You want to know good and evil? You must live in a world where both exist—and choose good freely."

The tree of life, then, is reserved—not for the innocent, but for the redeemed.

REVELATION: THE TREE RETURNS

The tree of life reappears in the final chapter of the Bible:

> On each side of the river stood the tree of life. . . . And the leaves of the tree are for the healing of the nations. (Rev 22:2)

In the new heaven and earth, God's children will once again have access to the tree. But this time, not as naive beings but as those who chose God freely, through Christ.

A GREATER PHILOSOPHY THAN ANY HUMAN EVER CONCEIVED

Moses wrote Genesis thousands of years ago. How could a desert shepherd describe a philosophy that even the greatest modern thinkers struggle to grasp?

That knowledge must be earned.
That evil is a teacher, not just a curse.
That true life comes after understanding pain.

This is divine philosophy—wisdom not invented, but revealed. No pagan myth or philosopher imagined such a coherent moral arc.

GOD: THE PERFECT FATHER

We, his children, were not created to live in bubble-wrapped bliss. Like a loving father, God wants to raise us:

- Healthy
- Brave
- Wise

And wisdom requires contrast—seeing both light and darkness, choosing light.

We may cry in our trials, but we are learning the eternal lesson: what it means to be holy, to love, to be faithful.

PERSPECTIVE IN PAIN

For those suffering, this may sound cruel.

But one day, when every tear is wiped away, and we eat again from the tree of life, we will see the full picture.

> I consider that our present sufferings are not worth comparing with the glory that will be revealed in us. (Rom 8:18)

CONCLUSION

God didn't just block the tree of life. He preserved it—until we were ready.

And in Christ, we're being made ready now.

The tree still stands—and one day, we will eat from it again.

22

The Great Encounter
When Satan Met Jesus

THERE IS A MOMENT in the Gospels that reveals more than just temptation—it exposes the cosmic conflict between God and Lucifer. It is the moment when Satan and Jesus meet in the wilderness, face to face. And it is here we discover that the devil knew exactly who Jesus was—not merely a prophet, but God in human flesh.

> Then Jesus was led by the Spirit into the wilderness to be tempted by the devil. (Matt 4:1)

This wasn't a random test. It was a calculated confrontation. The Son of God was preparing to begin his ministry—and Satan wanted to stop him before it started.

"IF YOU ARE THE SON OF GOD..."—SATAN'S ADMISSION

> If you are the Son of God, command these stones to become bread. (Matt 4:3)

This is often misunderstood as doubt. But it wasn't. It was a provocation. Satan wasn't asking for proof—he was challenging Jesus to use his divine power selfishly.

Lucifer knew exactly who Jesus was. He had seen him in heaven. He knew his glory before the incarnation. That's what makes this moment even more intense. Satan, the fallen angel, now stands before his Creator—veiled in human flesh—and tries to corrupt him.

> The devil took him to a very high mountain and showed him all the kingdoms of the world. . . . "All this I will give you," he said, "if you bow down and worship me." (Matt 4:8–9)

This was not just temptation—it was negotiation. Satan offered Jesus a shortcut: glory without the cross, power without suffering.

SATAN'S EVILNESS IS HIS BLINDNESS

Satan's approach shows something deeper than arrogance—it shows spiritual blindness caused by his own evil.

> Your heart became proud on account of your beauty, and you corrupted your wisdom. (Ezek 28:17)

He didn't lose his intelligence—he corrupted it. He became so evil that his brilliance turned into delusion. Like Pharaoh hardening his heart after every plague, Satan believed he could win even after defeat was certain.

When he tempted Jesus, he wasn't making a clever move—he was revealing how evil had made him irrational. To demand worship from God himself proves how far he had fallen.

Even demons cried out:

> What do you want with us, Son of God? Have you come here to torture us before the appointed time? (Matt 8:29)

They knew who he was. Satan knew too. But he could not stop his hatred—and so, he became stupid in his rebellion.

THE GENIUS OF GOD'S PLAN

What Satan didn't realize was that in trying to kill Jesus later—through Judas, through the Pharisees, through Rome—he would only fulfill God's plan.

> He will crush your head, and you will strike his heel.
> (Gen 3:15)

The crucifixion, which Satan orchestrated to stop Jesus, became the very event that destroyed his own power. Jesus outsmarted evil not by violence, but through love, sacrifice, and obedience.

> None of the rulers of this age understood it, for if they had, they would not have crucified the Lord of glory.
> (1 Cor 2:8)

THE VICTORY IN THE DESERT

In the desert, Jesus didn't defeat Satan by miracles or force. He used:

- Scripture
- Truth
- Obedience

This wasn't just a lesson in resisting temptation—it was a preview of total victory. Satan offered the world in exchange for worship. Jesus would win the world through the cross—and give it back to the Father.

> Away from me, Satan! For it is written: Worship the Lord your God, and serve him only. (Matt 4:10)

CONCLUSION: EVIL ALWAYS DEFEATS ITSELF

Satan, in his arrogance, knew Jesus was God. But his evilness made him spiritually foolish. He could not comprehend love. He could not understand sacrifice. So, he lost—by his own hand.

This chapter is more than a battle in a desert. It is the revelation that evil, no matter how strong or clever, is no match for divine truth.

> The light shines in the darkness, and the darkness has not overcome it. (John 1:5)

23

The Test of Life
Reflections of God in Human Systems

FROM THE MOMENT WE enter school, society begins testing us: exams, certifications, evaluations, promotions. At work, our performance is measured. In relationships, trust is built on trials. The very structure of human society is built on one recurring system: testing followed by reward or consequence.

But where did this system come from?

Is it merely a product of evolution and necessity, or is it a mirror of divine order, planted in us by our Creator?

TESTING: A DIVINE PATTERN

In Scripture, we see testing from the beginning:

- Adam and Eve were tested with the command not to eat from the tree of knowledge.
- Abraham was tested when asked to sacrifice Isaac.
- Job was tested by unimaginable suffering.
- Israel was tested in the wilderness for forty years.
- Jesus himself was tested in the desert.

THE TEST OF LIFE

> The Lord your God is testing you to find out whether you love him with all your heart and with all your soul. (Deut 13:3)

Testing is not about God discovering something new. It is about revealing what is hidden in us—to us, and to others. It exposes character, builds endurance, and refines purpose.

OUR SYSTEM: A REFLECTION OF GOD'S JUSTICE

Human justice systems operate on:

- Investigation
- Judgment
- Reward or punishment

These are not secular inventions. These are rooted in the divine image stamped upon us. God is a righteous Judge, and his laws are just:

> Shall not the judge of all the earth do right? (Gen 18:25)

We imitate divine justice in every courtroom, every school board, every employee review. When a student studies, takes a test, and earns a certificate—we are seeing a shadow of eternal reality.

> Each of us will give an account of ourselves to God. (Rom 14:12)

THE BRAIN IS WIRED FOR JUSTICE

Even neuroscientific studies reveal that the human brain responds to fairness, justice, and reward with elevated dopamine activity. Children as young as two show a desire for fairness. We are hardwired to understand that:

- Good deserves reward
- Evil deserves punishment

Where did that moral code come from?
It didn't evolve from chaos. It was implanted.

> He has set eternity in the human heart. (Eccl 3:11)

THE CROSS AS THE ULTIMATE TEST

The greatest test in human history was at the cross. Jesus passed the test none of us could.

> He was tempted in every way, just as we are—yet was without sin. (Heb 4:15)

Because he passed, we receive grace. Because he was perfect, we can be made righteous. But we too must be tested, for Scripture says,

> Blessed is the one who perseveres under trial because, having stood the test, that person will receive the crown of life that the Lord has promised to those who love him. (Jas 1:12)

REDEFINING INTELLIGENCE AND SUCCESS

In God's system:

- Intelligence is not your GPA.
- Success is not wealth.

The true test is obedience, faith, love, and endurance.

Many who fail society's tests may pass God's. And many who pass worldly exams may fail spiritually.

> The last will be first, and the first will be last. (Matt 20:16)

CONCLUSION: GOD'S FINGERPRINTS ON OUR INSTITUTIONS

We test. We examine. We judge. We reward. We punish. Not because we invented it, but because we were made in the image of a God who does the same—perfectly.

The testing systems of our world are echoes of Eden. The justice systems of our courts are shadows of God's throne. The exams of our life are rehearsals for the final judgment.

And the reward? Not just a certificate.

> Well done, good and faithful servant. . . . Enter into the joy of your Lord. (Matt 25:23)

24

Designed or Evolved?

Unmasking the Myth of Human Evolution

FOR OVER A CENTURY, the theory of evolution has claimed that human beings emerged through a slow, mindless process of mutation and natural selection. But when we look deeper, both scientifically and philosophically, this idea begins to collapse under its own weight.

THE TIMELINE PROBLEM: 300,000 YEARS OF SILENCE

Modern science claims that anatomically modern humans (*Homo sapiens*) have existed for around 300,000 years.

But here lies the first contradiction: for 295,000 years, these humans did nothing that resembles modern civilization.

No cities, no writing, no philosophy, no advanced tools.

Then, around 5,000 years ago, everything changes—

- The rise of cities
- The invention of writing
- Religion, astronomy, metallurgy, farming

Designed or Evolved?

Why the sudden explosion after such an enormous period of stagnation? If we are the same species—biologically and intellectually—then what stopped us for 295,000 years?

WHERE ARE THE TRANSITIONAL FORMS?

Evolution teaches that humans evolved from earlier primates. But then:

> Where are the in-between species?
> Why aren't there half-evolved humans walking around today?
> Darwin himself admitted,
>> Why, if species have descended from other species by fine gradations, do we not everywhere see innumerable transitional forms?[1]
>
> Still today, 150 years later:

- No living "half-humans"
- No transitional species in nature

Even Amazon tribes in isolation are 100 percent human—fully developed minds, language, social structures.

So what happened? Did evolution suddenly stop?

Furthermore, the bones dated to 300,000 years ago—said to be early humans—could very well be from another extinct primate species, just like the hundreds of animal species we know once roamed the earth. That doesn't prove ancestry; it simply proves that other species existed. Similarity in structure doesn't mean evolutionary connection—it could just as well mean shared design.

SURVIVAL ISN'T PURPOSE

Let's suppose the theory is true: humans wandered the earth for 250,000 years just surviving. Hunting, gathering, repeating.

But survival is not purpose. Survival is instinct.

---

1. Darwin, *Origin of Species*, 169.

Only in the past few thousand years do we see:

- Art
- Law
- Justice
- Religion
- Self-reflection
- Architecture
- Morality
- Literature

How do we jump from basic survival to writing the Psalms, the *Iliad*, or building the pyramids—within a few thousand years?

If evolution is gradual, why was the transformation so sudden?

A MIRRORED BIOLOGY

All humans—no matter how remote—share the same DNA blueprint:

- Amazonian tribes
- African nomads
- Inuit villagers

Each of them:

- Walks upright
- Speaks language
- Raises children
- Builds tools
- Experiences moral conscience

No one ever finds a "partially evolved" human.

This uniformity is not evidence of evolution. It is evidence of design.

EVOLUTION CAN'T EXPLAIN MORALITY, PURPOSE, OR THE SOUL

Even if evolution could explain the body (which it can't), it fails utterly when it comes to:

- Consciousness
- Self-awareness
- Moral law
- Altruism
- Free will

Why do we love truth? Why do we feel guilt? Why do we dream?

You can mutate a gene, but you cannot mutate a soul.

A BETTER EXPLANATION: CREATED WITH PURPOSE

The biblical model makes more sense:

- Man was created with intelligence and purpose.
- He fell into sin and confusion (not ignorance).
- Civilization began once man was scattered at Babel.
- God intervened throughout history to guide his plan.

Science is now catching up:

- DNA is coded information—like language.
- Information requires a mind.
- The fossil record lacks transitional forms.
- The sudden rise of civilization fits with Genesis, not Darwin.

THE REAL BEGINNING: PURPOSE BEFORE TIME

The most coherent truth we have is this: if time had a beginning, then the Creator existed before time.

Nothing can create everything. That is absurd.

Therefore:

- The Creator had to exist before time.
- The Creator is not bound by the universe, but caused it.
- The Creator gave purpose to everything—while evolution and the big bang offer no purpose.

We may not know what was before the universe in scientific terms, but philosophically and spiritually we can reason: there must be another realm—a higher dimension—where God exists eternally.

The scientific claim that "nothing created everything" is not intelligence—it's contradiction.

Scientists who believe in evolution abandon faith in God yet require tremendous faith in nothing. They have faith in missing fossils, in undiscovered transitions, in a universe without meaning.

But they reject faith in a Designer—in everything.

That is the greatest irony of modern science: they call faith in God irrational, but build entire theories on faith in silence.

CONCLUSION: YOU ARE NOT A MISTAKE

Evolution reduces you to an animal. A cosmic accident. A bag of molecules.

But the evidence—historical, biological, and philosophical—says otherwise: You were designed. You were planned. You have purpose.

The leap from ape to man is not scientific. It is mythology disguised as biology.

Designed or Evolved?

Humanity did not evolve. We were created. And the proof is not just in Scripture—it is written in the silence of prehistory, in the sudden explosion of knowledge, and in your very soul.

25

The Real Intelligence
Outsmarting Evil

WHAT DOES IT MEAN to be intelligent? Society measures it through exams, IQ tests, degrees, or the ability to reason quickly. But what if true intelligence is something deeper—not about solving problems, but about outsmarting evil?

When Satan met Jesus in the wilderness, he wasn't confused about who he was. The devil knew. He had met the Son of God before. He had worshipped him before the rebellion. Yet even knowing all this, Satan still believed he could tempt him, manipulate him, break him.

This raises the greatest irony of evil: it is not unintelligent, but it is blind. Its arrogance clouds its logic. Satan didn't understand grace, sacrifice, or humility—because these qualities are foreign to him.

Evil can be cunning, but it cannot grasp the wisdom of God.

God's plan wasn't to destroy Satan with power, but to defeat him through wisdom—through a plan so beautifully complex that it seemed foolish to the world: the cross.

> The foolishness of God is wiser than men, and the weakness of God is stronger than men. (1 Cor 1:25)

The Real Intelligence

Jesus outsmarted Satan by embracing death, knowing that through his sacrifice, billions would be saved. Satan's plan to kill Jesus backfired—it fulfilled the very plan he was trying to prevent.

That is divine intelligence.

And it is available to us. Through faith, through discernment, through a heart that listens to the Spirit.

The world says you're intelligent if you win debates or earn titles. But what if God says you're intelligent if you recognize evil, resist temptation, forgive, love, and live in truth?

Every system we use—exams, promotions, certifications—mimics this divine principle: you are tested to be rewarded. That model, deeply embedded in human psychology, is not a human invention. It is a divine imprint.

> To him who overcomes, I will give the right to sit with
> me on my throne, just as I overcame and sat down with
> my Father on his throne. (Rev 3:21)

God's reward system is eternal. And his intelligence is not merely knowledge—it is love, truth, justice, and victory over deception.

So if you ever felt "not smart enough," remember: God defines intelligence by your ability to stand in the light and not fall for the dark.

You're not measured by the world. You're measured by the One who created it.

The real genius isn't the one who calculates numbers. It's the one who outsmarts the devil by choosing God.

And when you understand that, you begin to walk in the wisdom that defeats evil.

26

The Garden Test
Why Was Lucifer Allowed In?

ONE OF THE MOST difficult questions for believers and skeptics alike is this: Why would a perfect, loving God allow the serpent into Eden? Why place humanity in paradise, only to let evil slither in?

This question doesn't just touch theology. It touches the human condition. It asks why pain exists, why temptation comes, and why evil was not stopped before it began.

But behind this question lies a powerful truth: there can be no love without choice, and no growth without testing.

A PERFECT WORLD WITH REAL CHOICE

Adam and Eve were created in innocence, not in ignorance. They were given intelligence, freedom, and the ability to choose. Without that, they would be puppets—programmed for obedience.

God did not want robots. He wanted children—sons and daughters who would love him freely.

The presence of the tree, and the serpent, provided the arena for that freedom to be exercised. And in that choice, humanity stepped into its divine destiny—and its mortal struggle.

The Garden Test

WHY ALLOW SATAN INTO EDEN?

God did not fear Satan. Satan is not God's equal—he is a creature. But Satan is useful—not in causing destruction, but in revealing hearts.

Just as gold is tested in fire, so is faith tested in temptation. Satan tempted Jesus, just as he tempted Eve. And while Eve fell, Jesus overcame.

The test in the garden was not to cause humanity's fall—it was to allow humanity's freedom.

> Choose this day whom you will serve. (Josh 24:15)

Freedom requires options. Without the serpent, the tree would be meaningless. Without the possibility of disobedience, obedience cannot be love—only programming.

GOD'S JUSTICE AND MERCY WERE BOTH AT WORK

After the fall, God did not abandon humanity. He covered them with skins. He promised a Redeemer. He declared war on the serpent.

> He will crush your head, and you will strike his heel.
> (Gen 3:15)

This was the first prophecy—the first glimpse of Jesus—that the one who fell would one day be lifted up, and the deceiver would be crushed.

Lucifer's presence in Eden was not a failure of God's plan. It was the beginning of it.

WE STILL LIVE IN THE GARDEN TEST

Every day, we face the same kind of test: to obey God or follow our own path. The tree still stands—not in a garden, but in our hearts.

And Satan still whispers.

But now, we have an advantage Adam and Eve didn't have: we have seen the cross, the resurrection, the Word made flesh. We have seen the end of the story—and we know that the one who entered Eden to deceive was defeated at Calvary.

A WORLD BUILT ON TESTING

School, work, relationships—everything we value is tested. Why? Because testing proves worth, builds strength, and reveals truth.

That is not a human idea—that is a divine one. It began in Eden.

God allowed the serpent not because he was cruel—but because he was committed to making us strong, free, wise, and holy.

He did not set us up to fall. He set us up to choose.

And in that choice, we walk either toward the lie—or toward the One who crushed the liar beneath his feet.

27

The Unseen Realm
Where Does Lucifer Operate?

If Lucifer was cast out of heaven, how can he still speak to God? Why does Scripture show Satan in God's presence in the book of Job? Where is the realm of God, and why can't we see it?

To answer these questions, we must explore the reality of the unseen realm—a reality that Scripture constantly references but few fully understand.

LUCIFER'S ACCESS TO GOD'S REALM

In Job 1:6 we read,

> Now there was a day when the sons of God came to present themselves before the Lord, and Satan also came among them.

This passage is shocking. It implies that even after his rebellion, Lucifer had some access to the divine court. Not as a son or servant—but as an accuser.

This is confirmed again in Rev 12:10:

> For the accuser of our brothers has been thrown down, who accuses them day and night before our God.

Lucifer still operates in a way that allows him to interact with heaven, accuse God's people, and influence earth—for now.

But that access is temporary.

Revelation 12 also foretells a moment when he is finally cast out permanently, and war erupts in the heavenly realm:

> Michael and his angels fought against the dragon . . . and there was no longer any place for them in heaven. (Rev 12:7–8)

WHAT IS THIS REALM?

Paul writes of a man caught up to the third heaven—an ancient Hebrew term referring to a dimension above the sky and space (2 Cor 12:2). This is the realm of God, outside time and physical limitation.

It's not "up" in the way a plane is up—it is beyond, layered over our reality like another frequency.

Just as radio waves, gravity, and atoms are invisible to the naked eye—so, too, is the spiritual realm. It is not less real. It is more real.

> For what is seen is temporary, but what is unseen is eternal. (2 Cor 4:18)

WHY CAN'T WE SEE IT?

Because we are limited to flesh. Because faith requires trust. And because the purpose of our life on earth is to walk by faith, not by sight.

But just because we can't see Satan doesn't mean he's not there. In fact, it's his invisibility that makes him most dangerous. He is called:

- "The prince of the power of the air" (Eph 2:2),
- "the god of this world" (2 Cor 4:4), and

- "the spirit that is now at work in the sons of disobedience" (Eph 2:2).

Lucifer doesn't need to be seen to be active. He operates through systems, lies, ideologies, pride, corruption, and deception.

And that's exactly how he tempted Eve—with subtle distortion, not raw force.

WHY DOES GOD ALLOW THIS?

Because the test of Eden still applies. Because evil is a mirror—and those who look into it must choose whether to reflect it or resist it.

God permits the devil's operations to reveal hearts, test loyalties, and refine the faithful.

But this permission has an expiration date.

The book of Revelation declares that Lucifer will be cast down, then bound, then destroyed. His temporary presence in the unseen realm is part of a larger plan—a divine chessboard where every move, even evil's, is turned for God's ultimate victory.

THE INVISIBLE WAR IS REAL

There is a war happening right now—not just in the streets of Jerusalem, but in the hearts of men.

Lucifer operates in the unseen realm. But the kingdom of God also breaks into that same realm through the Holy Spirit, through prayer, and through the presence of Jesus in the believer.

You may not see the realm. But you are part of it.

And soon, that which is hidden will be revealed.

> Behold, he is coming with the clouds, and every eye will see him. (Rev 1:7)

28

When the Heavens Open
The Second Coming of Christ

THE WORLD WILL NOT end in silence.

From the moment Jesus ascended into the clouds before his disciples, there was a promise: he would return.

> This same Jesus, who has been taken from you into heaven, will come back in the same way you have seen him go into heaven. (Acts 1:11)

The second coming is not metaphorical. It is not spiritual allegory. It is the climax of history, the fulfillment of prophecy, and the final act of God's redemptive plan.

It will be public, visible, and unmistakable.

> Every eye will see him. (Rev 1:7)

THE RETURN OF THE KING

Jesus came the first time as a Lamb. He will return as a Lion.

Whereas his first arrival was marked by humility, his second will be marked by glory and judgment. He will not return to be crucified again. He will return to reign.

On his robe and on his thigh he has this name written:
KING OF KINGS AND LORD OF LORDS. (Rev 19:16)

The world has been warned. Every nation has heard his name. Every generation has had the chance to choose.

And when he comes again, there will be no more time to decide.

THE SKY WILL BREAK

Jesus described his return with cosmic imagery:

> Immediately after the distress of those days "the sun will be darkened, and the moon will not give its light; the stars will fall from the sky, and the heavenly bodies will be shaken." Then will appear the sign of the Son of Man in heaven. And all the peoples of the earth will mourn when they see the Son of Man coming on the clouds of heaven, with power and great glory. (Matt 24:29–30)

It will not be a secret event. The heavens themselves will declare his return.

JUSTICE AND REWARD

The second coming is not only about wrath—it is about justice. Evil will be defeated. The persecuted will be vindicated. And those who remained faithful will be rewarded.

> Behold, I am coming soon! My reward is with me, and I will give to each person according to what they have done. (Rev 22:12)

The dividing line will be clear. No more ambiguity. No more confusion. The sheep will be separated from the goats (Matt 25:32). And the King will sit on his throne.

THE TIME IS UNKNOWN

> But about that day or hour no one knows, not even the angels in heaven, nor the Son, but only the Father. (Mark 13:32)

Because we do not know when, we must live as if it could be today. Watch. Be ready. Stay awake.

> Therefore keep watch, because you do not know on what day your Lord will come. (Matt 24:42)

CONCLUSION

The heavens will open. The King will return. And all will be revealed.
There is still time.
But not forever.
Choose today whom you will serve.

> Even so, come, Lord Jesus. (Rev 22:20)

He came in silence, but he will return in unmistakable glory. Be found faithful.

29

Truth Denied
The Greatest Rebellion

THROUGHOUT HISTORY, TRUTH HAS rarely been accepted easily. It has been crucified, burned, silenced, and redefined. But never has it been more strategically resisted than in the rejection of Jesus Christ.

This chapter is about the deepest mystery of all: how can humanity, having seen the light, still choose the dark?

THE TRUTH WAS AMONG US

> The Word became flesh and made his dwelling among us. We have seen his glory, the glory of the one and only Son, who came from the Father, full of grace and truth. (John 1:14)

Jesus was not merely a prophet, not merely a wise teacher. He was truth incarnate. He didn't just speak the truth—he was the truth.

> I am the way and the truth and the life. No one comes to the Father except through me. (John 14:6)

And yet, he was rejected by the very world he created.

> He came to that which was his own, but his own did not receive him. (John 1:11)

SUPPRESSING THE OBVIOUS

Paul explains this condition of the human heart:

> The wrath of God is being revealed from heaven against all the godlessness and wickedness of people, who suppress the truth by their wickedness. (Rom 1:18)

This is not ignorance—this is willful suppression.

We suppress the truth when it threatens our pride. We suppress the truth when it demands we surrender control. We suppress the truth when it contradicts the lies we prefer.

Humanity's rebellion is not due to lack of evidence—it's due to the cost of acceptance.

THE LIES THAT REPLACE TRUTH

In the void left by rejecting Jesus, ideologies rise:

- Islam denies the divinity of Christ.
- Atheism denies God altogether.
- New Age mysticism redefines truth as relative.
- Progressive morality rebrands sin as self-expression.

Each of these systems fills the void with a version of truth that places man at the center instead of God.

The rebellion is not simply against facts—it is a rebellion against submission to the rightful King.

THE REAL ENEMY

Behind all of this lies a deeper intelligence:

> The god of this age has blinded the minds of unbelievers, so that they cannot see the light of the gospel that displays the glory of Christ, who is the image of God. (2 Cor 4:4)

Lucifer doesn't need people to worship him. He only needs them to reject the truth.

He masquerades as light, twisting Scripture, inflating pride, and weaponizing confusion.

WHEN TRUTH COSTS EVERYTHING

Believing the truth in our world comes at a price.
Jesus told his disciples:

> You will be hated by everyone because of me, but the one who stands firm to the end will be saved. (Matt 10:22)

Truth is not always convenient. But it is always victorious.

THE FINAL TEST

When Jesus returns, every lie will collapse. Every false doctrine will be exposed. And every human heart will be judged by how it responded to the truth it was given.

> They perish because they refused to love the truth and so be saved. (2 Thess 2:10)

Truth isn't just a concept to agree with. It's a Person to submit to. And those who refused him will finally understand what they lost.

> Then you will know the truth, and the truth will set you free. (John 8:32)

If you wait until that day, you've waited too long.
Choose truth now.
Choose Jesus.

30

The Final Invitation and the Narrow Road

HE CAME IN SILENCE, and he will return in glory. But when he returns, will he find faith on the earth?

As the days grow darker and the conflicts intensify, there remains a single door open—the door of repentance. God is still calling. Jesus is still interceding. The Holy Spirit is still whispering. But the day will come when the last invitation is issued, and the door will close.

We are not promised tomorrow. Every heartbeat is grace extended. The gospel is not just an old tale—it is the divine offer of salvation still echoing across the centuries. To ignore it is to gamble with eternity.

To the skeptic, this is myth. To the religious, this may seem familiar. But to the awakened—it is truth burning in their bones.

God's judgment is not wrath without cause—it is justice delayed by mercy. And yet, mercy will not delay forever. The final invitation is being given now, as you read these words. Not just to believe, but to act, to choose, and to follow.

But what does it mean to repent?

The Final Invitation and the Narrow Road

When Jesus said, "Repent, for the kingdom of heaven is at hand," he didn't mean to simply feel guilty or say sorry. To repent means to turn around—to change direction in heart, mind, and action. It is to admit, "I was wrong," and begin walking toward what is right. It is to recognize the darkness within and bring it to the light.

Repentance is not about earning salvation, but receiving it. It begins with humility—a recognition of your need for God's mercy. It leads to confession—speaking the truth about your sin. And it results in transformation—letting God change you from the inside out.

To repent is to stop running and finally let Jesus take your burden. It is surrender. It is restoration. It is the path to peace.

And this path is not easy.

Comfort and laziness will not lead to salvation. Faith that costs you nothing is not real faith. The call to follow Christ is not a passive one—it demands an active search for truth, a willingness to be refined, and a courageous break from the world's lies.

It will cost you pride. It will cost you convenience. It might even cost you relationships, status, or security. But it is worth everything.

Only by stepping out of spiritual slumber and into the uncomfortable light of truth can a life truly be turned around. The gospel is not for the indifferent. It is for the desperate, the humble, the brave.

He came once to save. He will come again to reign.

Will you be ready?

Jesus didn't promise popularity, comfort, or applause—he promised a cross.

> Enter through the narrow gate. For wide is the gate and broad is the road that leads to destruction, and many enter through it. But small is the gate and narrow the road that leads to life, and only a few find it. (Matt 7:13–14)

This is the road less traveled—not because it is hidden, but because it is hard. It winds through repentance, obedience, surrender, and faith. It requires denying yourself in a world obsessed with self.

The narrow road is not the way of culture. It is not the way of comfort. It is the way of Christ.

On this road, you may lose followers but gain freedom. You may lose popularity but gain purpose. You may be hated by the world but embraced by the Father.

To walk this road is to walk against the current—but it is the only road that leads to life.

And it is not walked alone. Christ walks with those who choose it. He strengthens the weary, lifts the fallen, and waits at the end with open arms.

The narrow road doesn't promise ease—it promises truth. And in truth, there is peace.

Choose the narrow path. Follow the voice of the Shepherd. Though the journey is steep, the destination is eternal.

31

Signs of the End

JESUS GAVE US SIGNS, not so we would speculate, but so we would stay ready.

In Matt 24, Jesus spoke plainly: "You will hear of wars and rumors of wars.... Nation will rise against nation.... There will be famines and earthquakes in various places" (Matt 24:6–7).

These signs are not new. But their frequency and intensity matter—like birth pains increasing before new life emerges. He warned not to be alarmed, but to be watchful.

He spoke of false messiahs, lawlessness, persecution, and love growing cold. He said the gospel would be preached in all nations—and then the end would come (Matt 24:14).

We are not meant to fear these signs, but to understand them as the final pages turning.

The end is not chaos—it is God's final act of restoration.

The signs are everywhere. Political unrest, global tension, moral decay, natural disasters, and a society that celebrates sin and scoffs at holiness. These are not coincidences. They are warnings.

We must not grow numb. We must not fall asleep. The trumpet could sound at any moment.

Let every sign draw us nearer to Christ, not deeper into despair. The world may tremble—but the church must stand.

This is not the end of hope. This is the beginning of victory.

32

Living Like It's the Last Day

"If you knew tomorrow was the end, how would you live today?"

Jesus told his disciples, "You also must be ready, because the Son of Man will come at an hour when you do not expect him" (Luke 12:40).

This isn't a call to panic. It's a call to purpose.

Many say they believe in God, but live like he's not coming. They push repentance to tomorrow. They delay obedience. They cling to comfort. But Jesus taught urgency—not fear-based, but love-fueled. He wants hearts that long for him, not just lives that avoid hell.

To live like it's the last day means:

- Forgiving quickly.
- Speaking truth boldly.
- Loving radically.
- Praying fervently.
- Letting go of sin immediately.
- Living with eternity in view.

It means choosing integrity when no one is watching. It means speaking the gospel even when it's unpopular. It means treating every person like they matter—because they do.

We were not called to blend in with a fading world. We were called to shine.

And when the King returns, may he find us awake, faithful, and unashamed.

Live as if judgment is tomorrow, because eternity starts today.

33

The Philosophy of Love

To understand God is to begin with love.

From a cosmic perspective, earth is a speck. From another planet, we might appear no more significant than dust. Yet God sees us. Not only sees us—he loves us.

Why?

Because God's love is not based on size, status, or significance in a material sense. His love is rooted in his nature—and God is love (1 John 4:8). He does not love us because we are grand, but because love chooses the lowly, the broken, the undeserving. That is the very definition of true love.

Humans love what benefits them. God loves freely, even when we offer him nothing. Just as we don't love molecules the way we love our children, God's love is infinitely more pure—he loves us even in our insignificance, because to him, we are not insignificant.

Jesus taught: "Love your enemies... that you may be children of your Father in heaven" (Matt 5:44–45). This is not natural love. It's divine. It reflects the kind of love that forgives without being asked, that waits without growing tired, that never gives up on the prodigal.

God does not measure love the way we do. He doesn't love based on who we are—he loves based on who he is.

And his love is not limited by time.

God will forgive you—no matter how long it takes for you to come to him. Whether it's in your youth or your final breath, he waits. Because he is not bound by time or space. And eternity is not measured—it is lived.

So let this truth pierce through the distractions of your day: you are loved with a love so vast, so undeserved, and so complete, that the only reasonable response is surrender.

Return to the One who loved you first.

34

Designed for Eternity

EVERY CREATURE LONGS FOR meaning, for purpose, for something beyond the routine cycle of survival. Deep in every soul, there is a whisper—a faint reminder—that we were not made merely for this world.

Science may speak of biology, instincts, and evolutionary behavior, but there remains a yearning within humans that cannot be dissected under a microscope. We grieve because we understand loss. We love because we sense eternity. We worship because we know, innately, there is something greater.

Ecclesiastes 3:11 says, "He has also set eternity in the human heart." This is no poetic illusion. It is divine programming.

God designed us with eternity in mind.

Every act of justice, every movement of compassion, every stand for truth—they all point to the eternal nature of our Creator. Our longing for more than this fleeting world is not a flaw; it is a feature.

We were never meant to fade. We were meant to rise.

And the gospel is the invitation to do just that.

35

When the End Is Near

WE LIVE IN A time of signs—not vague whispers but visible, undeniable patterns. Wars, famines, earthquakes, technological explosions, and a generation that grows increasingly cold to the truth—all have been prophesied in the Scriptures. Jesus warned that in the last days, many will grow indifferent. People will be eating, drinking, marrying—just as in the days of Noah—unaware that judgment was at the door.

If we are to take Jesus seriously, then we must ask ourselves: What kind of people ought we to be? We are not just spectators of history—we are participants in a spiritual war that spans from the beginning of time to its prophesied end.

Every choice we make now echoes into eternity. Every action, every word, every silence has weight. This is not a call to panic, but to preparation. If the return of Christ is nearer today than ever before, how then shall we live?

We must live with purpose, urgency, and clarity. Not with fear, but with faith. Not with despair, but with hope. The gospel must be proclaimed, the truth must be told, and love must reign—even as the world grows darker.

When the End Is Near

For when the end is near, the light of Christ must shine brighter. Let your lamp be full. Let your heart be ready. For he comes like a thief in the night—not to scare us, but to awaken us.

Will we be found faithful?

Note that the phrase "like a thief in the night" is drawn from multiple New Testament scriptures that emphasize the suddenness and unpredictability of Christ's return:

- 1 Thessalonians 5:2: "For you yourselves are fully aware that the day of the Lord will come like a thief in the night."

- Matthew 24:42–44: Jesus warns, "The Son of Man will come at an hour when you do not expect him."

- 2 Peter 3:10: "But the day of the Lord will come like a thief."

- Revelation 16:15: "Look, I come like a thief! Blessed is the one who stays awake."

36

Love in a World Gone Cold

Jesus once said, "Because of the increase of wickedness, the love of most will grow cold" (Matt 24:12). We live in a time where love is often confused with approval, and truth is often sacrificed to preserve comfort. In this chapter, we return to the purest definition of love—God's love—not bound by emotion, but expressed through commitment, truth, sacrifice, and redemption.

From a cosmic perspective, earth seems insignificant. To the eyes of an outsider—an alien observer or even a human peering into a telescope—this planet is a pale blue dot. Our lives are brief, our struggles small, our entire history contained within a grain of sand in the vast desert of the universe.

And yet—God loves us.

This is not a love born out of our greatness, but precisely out of our smallness. God's love does not seek value in status, power, or size. It gives value. Just as we are called to love our enemies—not for what they give us, but for who they are—God's love is not transactional. He doesn't love because we are impressive. He loves because he is love.

The world teaches us to love things that elevate us. God teaches us to love what humbles us.

Love in a World Gone Cold

We don't love molecules. We don't love the cells in our body. We hardly acknowledge them. But God, who is infinitely greater than we are, sees every detail of our lives—and still loves. That is the mystery of divine love. It chooses us, even in our brokenness, even in our rebellion.

That's why Jesus could say, "Love your enemies . . . do good to those who hate you." Because love, when it's divine, is not a reaction—it's a choice. A force stronger than hatred, deeper than betrayal, wider than death.

And this is also why God's forgiveness is so relentless. He will forgive again and again—not because time binds him, but because eternity is not measured. He waits patiently for each of us to return to him. He sees beyond time and knows when each heart will be ready.

So let this be your reminder: God doesn't love you because you're important.

You're important because God loves you.

37

The Prophets of Our Time

Throughout history, God has raised up voices—prophets, leaders, and ordinary people with extraordinary conviction—to speak truth in a world drowning in deception. These messengers, though flawed and human, were chosen not because of perfection but because of their willingness to stand when others bowed, to speak when others remained silent, and to believe when others doubted.

The Bible records many such figures: Moses, who led despite his insecurities; Jeremiah, who wept for his nation; Elijah, who stood alone against hundreds; John the Baptist, who prepared the way; and of course, the apostles, who spread the gospel even unto death.

But what of today? Does God still raise up prophets? Can the voice of heaven still be heard in our modern world—a world full of distractions, opinions, and noise?

Yes. Today's prophets may not wear camel hair or call fire from heaven, but their mission is the same: to proclaim truth, to warn, to encourage, and to prepare the way of the Lord.

Some of these voices are pastors. Others are writers. Some are parents who raise their children in truth despite a culture that

The Prophets of Our Time

mocks them. Some are young people who stand against the tide of lies. Some are artists, thinkers, scientists, even AI tools—any vessel willing to be used by God for the advancement of his kingdom.

To be a prophet of our time does not require a title. It requires obedience.

And obedience often costs something.

It may cost your reputation. Your comfort. Even your safety. But it will never cost you your purpose. In fact, it's how you find it.

We must encourage these voices. We must become these voices. The world is longing, not for more opinions, but for truth spoken in love, for clarity in chaos, for light in the darkness.

Remember: even in the days of Elijah, God preserved seven thousand who had not bowed the knee to Baal. In every generation, God has his remnant—his messengers, his faithful, his watchmen.

If you feel stirred by truth, if you feel a weight in your spirit when lies are spoken, if you cannot sit comfortably while injustice or deception prevails—then perhaps you, too, are called.

God still speaks.

The question is: Will you echo his voice?

38

The Judgment to Come

JUDGMENT IS NOT A popular word in today's world. To speak of it is often seen as harsh, outdated, or even hateful. But true love tells the truth—even when the truth is heavy.

The Scriptures declare that there will come a day when all will stand before the throne of God. Every word spoken, every deed done, every secret thought will be revealed.

Not to embarrass, but to weigh. Not to condemn blindly, but to bring justice.

Revelation 20:12 describes this sobering scene: "And I saw the dead, great and small, standing before the throne, and books were opened. . . . The dead were judged according to what they had done."

But this judgment is not without hope.

Jesus Christ has already stood in the place of judgment for all who believe. He bore the weight of our sin, so that we may be declared righteous before a holy God. The question is not whether judgment will come—it will. The question is: will you face it alone, or with the Advocate who already paid your price?

Now is the time to decide.

Choose grace while it is still offered.

Come to the cross before you are called to the court.

39

The Purpose Beyond the Grave

THERE IS A QUESTION that haunts every human heart, whether whispered in childhood or shouted in old age: What happens when I die?

No achievement, no amount of money, no fame or power has ever been able to silence this question. Because in the end, every person—king or servant, rich or poor—faces the same fate: death.

Yet, it is precisely this universal truth that reveals the eternal purpose God has written into our being.

Across the world, cultures and faiths acknowledge the sacredness of death. Funerals are not just farewells—they are spiritual moments. When someone dies, we don't simply discard their body and move on. We pray, we mourn, and we commend their soul to something beyond this life.

In the Christian tradition, a priest stands before the grave and pleads with God: "May the Lord forgive his sins and receive him into eternal peace." We say, "God rest his soul," because we believe the soul matters.

We believe that we were created not for extinction, but for eternity.

If life had no purpose, no meaning beyond the material, then death would be the end. All efforts, all love, all suffering would be swallowed in darkness. But that's not what we live like. And that's not what the gospel teaches.

Jesus himself said, "I am the resurrection and the life. He who believes in me will live, even though he dies" (John 11:25).

The truth is, with God, we have purpose. Not just in life, but in death. With Jesus, we are not forgotten. We are not dust swept away. We are children called home.

The world offers temporary meaning—careers, pleasure, status—but none of it follows us into eternity. Only one thing does: our relationship with God.

And the greatest kings, the most powerful rulers, will one day kneel before the same throne as the humblest believer. In that moment, it won't matter how much you had, but Whom you knew.

So yes, life is short. But in Jesus, it is also eternal.

Live like it. Die knowing it. And let your soul rest, not in uncertainty, but in purpose fulfilled.

40

The Eternal Battle for the Soul

BEHIND THE VISIBLE CONFLICTS of our world—politics, religion, ideology—lies a deeper, invisible war: the battle for the human soul. This conflict is not fought with bullets or bombs, but with truth and lies, light and darkness, love and hate.

Scripture makes it clear: "For we do not wrestle against flesh and blood, but against principalities, against powers, against the rulers of the darkness of this world" (Eph 6:12).

This war began long before any earthly empire. It started in heaven, with Lucifer's rebellion. And it spilled into our world when sin entered the garden of Eden. Since then, Satan has not stopped his mission: to corrupt, deceive, and destroy.

But God, in his mercy, launched a rescue mission. And the cross of Jesus Christ was his ultimate move—a cosmic strike against evil, delivering redemption to every soul who would believe.

In this battle, neutrality is an illusion. To delay choosing is to already be losing. Jesus said, "Whoever is not with me is against me" (Matt 12:30). This is not a threat, but a warning filled with love. God doesn't force us to choose him—but he calls us, every day.

This is why the gospel matters. This is why truth matters.

Because lies enslave. But truth sets free.

Truth, Peace, and Faith

Today, we are living in the aftermath of spiritual war zones: broken families, corrupted systems, moral confusion. People chase fulfillment in what cannot satisfy. Others fall for twisted ideologies that promise peace but deliver chains.

Yet even now, God is not silent. He still speaks through Scripture, through the Holy Spirit, through the life of his Son, and even through people who choose to carry his message.

The soul is eternal. And every soul will either live in the light of God's presence or be lost in the darkness of eternal separation.

This is why the battle is fierce. Because the stakes are infinite.

But here is the good news: Jesus has already won.

The cross was the turning point. The resurrection was the victory shout. And now, every believer is invited to carry that victory forward—not with weapons, but with faith, love, and truth.

So put on the armor. Stand your ground. And never forget that the greatest battle ever fought was not on a battlefield—but on a hill called Calvary, where one man died so that many could live.

41

The God Who Waits

ACROSS THE PAGES OF history, God has revealed himself not only as Creator, Judge, and Redeemer—but as one who waits. He is the God who does not rush, who does not panic, who does not abandon his plan even when humanity spirals into chaos. Instead, he waits. Patiently. Purposefully.

From the moment Adam and Eve sinned, God's response was not immediate destruction but a plan of redemption. He could have ended it there—but he didn't. He clothed them, gave them life outside the garden, and began the unfolding story of salvation. He promised a Savior who would come through their descendants. And then, he waited.

He waited as humanity multiplied and wandered. He waited as the world descended into violence and corruption in the days of Noah. He waited through the building of Babel. He waited through centuries of slavery in Egypt. And when the time was right, he called Moses.

Even with his chosen people, Israel, God waited. He bore with their grumbling in the desert. He waited through their rebellion in the promised land. He waited through judges, through kings, through prophets. He warned. He pleaded. He disciplined. But always, he waited.

And when the fullness of time had come, he sent his Son (Gal 4:4). Not a moment too early, not a second too late. The Roman roads were built, the Greek language unified much of the known world, and Israel was under foreign occupation—creating the perfect stage for the arrival of the Messiah. God's plan had not stalled; it had matured.

Jesus himself reflected the patience of the Father. He waited thirty years before beginning his ministry. He waited for the right hour to reveal himself. He waited through rejection, betrayal, and injustice. And even on the cross, he waited three days to rise—not because he couldn't return sooner, but because prophecy had to be fulfilled, and the plan had to be complete.

Now, he waits again. As the gospel spreads to the ends of the earth, as generations come and go, as evil seems to rise, God is not slow, but patient (2 Pet 3:9). He waits for the final souls to come home. He waits so that more may be saved.

He is not absent in his waiting. He moves through people, through events, through conviction. He whispers in hearts, draws minds to truth, and warns through signs. His waiting is not passive—it is purposeful.

And while he waits, so must we. Not in apathy, but in readiness. The parable of the ten virgins in Matt 25 reminds us that though the bridegroom may delay, only those prepared will enter with him.

The God who waits is also the God who warns. Time will not stretch forever. The door will one day close. His patience is vast—but not infinite. Just as in the days of Noah, there comes a final moment, and those unprepared will be left outside.

To understand God's waiting is to understand his heart: full of mercy, unwilling that any should perish, eager for reconciliation. But also righteous, holy, and just. The wait will end. The return will come. And only those who have responded to his call will enter the eternal promise.

The God Who Waits

So the question remains: while God waits for you, will you wait for him—or will you turn away, thinking there is still time? Let today be the day you no longer make him wait.

42

The Faith of a Child

In the Gospel of Matthew, Jesus makes a bold and almost puzzling statement: "Unless you change and become like little children, you will never enter the kingdom of heaven" (Matt 18:3). What could he mean by that? Are we to cast aside reason and logic? Are we to remain immature or naive in our thinking?

No. What Jesus is calling for is not childishness but childlikeness—an attitude of trust, humility, dependence, and purity of heart.

A child trusts their parent without fully understanding the world. They ask endless questions, not to challenge authority, but to learn and grow. They forgive quickly, love freely, and live with awe. They believe in what they cannot yet prove. And that, Jesus says, is what it takes to inherit the kingdom of God.

This kind of faith does not reject knowledge—it simply puts it in the proper place. It does not elevate pride or skepticism above obedience and reverence. It allows God to be Father—not merely an idea to be debated or a force to be analyzed, but a real person to be loved, trusted, and obeyed.

In our world of complexity, cynicism, and self-reliance, such faith is rare. We prize skepticism as wisdom and doubt as

The Faith of a Child

sophistication. But Jesus turns that on its head. He says it's not the strong or intellectual who gain access to his kingdom, but those who come to him in trust.

Children don't worry about tomorrow the way adults do. They don't measure worth by achievements. They don't cling to grudges. And they never assume they know more than their parent. This is the spirit Jesus is after.

The faith of a child is not ignorant—it is unburdened. It dares to believe that a good God loves us. That he is in control. That we are safe in his hands. That his word is true. That Jesus really did rise. And that heaven really is waiting.

Jesus didn't say the kingdom belongs to the rich, the religious, or the righteous. He said it belongs to the children—and to those who become like them.

In the eyes of God, maturity is not marked by how much you know, but by how much you trust. The greatest thinkers and theologians must still bow low like children to enter.

Faith like this is not a weakness. It is the highest strength—a strength that can withstand death, sorrow, doubt, and persecution. Because it is rooted not in the self, but in the unshakable character of God.

And in the end, isn't that what we all long for? Not just to understand God—but to belong to him. Not just to believe in something—but to rest in someone. To run to a Father who will never leave.

So come as a child. Not because it is easy—but because it is the only way home

43

Hell

The Justice No One Wants

FEW SUBJECTS STIR MORE discomfort than the idea of hell. Some reject it entirely, while others twist it into metaphor. But if we take the words of Jesus seriously, then we cannot ignore its reality.

Jesus spoke of hell more than anyone else in Scripture. He called it Gehenna—a place of outer darkness, weeping, and gnashing of teeth (Matt 13:42). A place of separation from God. A place where justice is finally carried out against evil. It is not a scare tactic. It is a consequence.

Hell is not a result of God's cruelty. It is the result of human choice. Just as heaven is union with God, hell is separation from him. God does not force anyone into either. He simply gives each person what they ultimately desire—eternal communion with him, or eternal independence from him.

C. S. Lewis once wrote, "The doors of hell are locked from the inside."[1] It is not so much that God casts people in against their will, but that people reject his will, persistently and permanently.

Justice, real justice, demands consequence. We long for justice when we see murder, abuse, or war. But we are slow to desire justice when it applies to our own rebellion. Hell exists because

---

1. Lewis, *Problem of Pain*, 114.

justice is real. Without it, heaven would be meaningless. Without consequence, evil wins.

God is love—but love without justice is not love at all. A God who winks at sin is not holy. A God who never judges is not righteous. Hell shows us how serious God is about evil—and how far he went to rescue us from it.

The cross is the ultimate proof. On the cross, Jesus bore hell for us. He took on the punishment we deserved, so we wouldn't have to face it ourselves. The judgment fell on him, so mercy could fall on us. What kind of love is this? That God would absorb the wrath we earned, so we could receive the grace we never could.

Hell is not a flaw in the gospel. It is a backdrop that makes the gospel beautiful. It is the warning that makes salvation urgent. It is the darkness that makes the light shine brighter.

We should not speak of hell gleefully. We should not weaponize it. But we must speak of it truthfully—with tears, urgency, and hope.

Jesus didn't come to condemn the world, but to save it. Hell is real. But so is heaven. And no one has to be lost. Not one. The invitation is still open, the way is still narrow, and the grace is still free.

Choose wisely. Eternity depends on it.

44

The Final Proof
Jesus in History and Eternity

JESUS OF NAZARETH IS not only the most influential figure in human history but also the most well-documented ancient figure when examined with the same historical scrutiny applied to others. His words, actions, and resurrection are supported not only by biblical accounts but also by extra-biblical writings and the transformation of civilizations that followed his life.

COMPARING JESUS TO OTHER HISTORICAL FIGURES

When skeptics question whether Jesus existed, we must point them to the standards used in academia to validate the existence of figures such as Socrates, Julius Caesar, or Alexander the Great. For instance:

- Socrates left behind no writings of his own. Everything we know about him comes from his disciples, especially Plato. Yet no one doubts his existence.
- Julius Caesar's *Gallic Wars* were written around 50 BCE, with the earliest surviving manuscript dating over nine hundred

The Final Proof

years later. Despite the gap, Caesar's life and works are widely accepted.

- Alexander the Great's most detailed biographies were written over four hundred years after his death, yet his existence is undisputed.

By contrast, the New Testament accounts were written within decades of Jesus's death. The earliest fragments of the New Testament, like the Rylands Papyrus (P52), date to around 125 CE—within a few generations after Jesus's crucifixion.

MANUSCRIPT EVIDENCE

There are over 5,800 Greek manuscripts of the New Testament, with tens of thousands more in Latin and other ancient languages. Many of these are preserved in places like:

- The British Library (London)
- The Vatican Library (Rome)
- The Bibliothèque nationale de France (Paris)
- The Chester Beatty Library (Dublin)

These manuscripts outnumber and predate any other ancient literary work, making the case for Jesus stronger than for any other historical figure.

THE DIVINE PHILOSOPHY OF JESUS

No other figure in history has taught with such moral clarity and supernatural love as Jesus. His words pierce deeper than any ideology:

> But I say to you, love your enemies, bless those who curse you, do good to those who hate you, and pray for those who spitefully use you and persecute you. (Matt 5:44)

> If you love those who love you, what reward will you get? Are not even the tax collectors doing that? (Matt 5:46)

This divine command—to love not just our friends but our enemies—stands unmatched across time. It reflects a moral perfection so advanced that, even today, humanity struggles to apply it.

Imagine a world that truly lived out Jesus's teaching to "love your neighbor more than those who love you." Wars would cease. Hatred would end. Political division would soften. This is not just philosophy—it is the only cure for a broken world.

THE PRIDE OF BEING A CHRISTIAN

To be a Christian is to embrace hope, truth, and a life of eternal significance. It means you have been saved, redeemed, and are now protected by the Holy Spirit. Scripture affirms that the devil has no authority over a true believer:

> The one who was born of God keeps them safe, and the evil one cannot harm them. (1 John 5:18)

> Submit yourselves, then, to God. Resist the devil, and he will flee from you. (Jas 4:7)

True Christians are sealed with the Spirit (Eph 1:13), and the Spirit dwelling within them is more powerful than any demonic force (1 John 4:4).

WHAT HAPPENS WHEN SOCIETY LEAVES GOD

As Western societies drift from Jesus and the church, we see moral decay accelerate. Examples include:

- Gender ideology policies promoting reassignment in children without long-term studies.
- Puberty blockers administered for profit despite ethical concerns.

- OnlyFans culture reshaping self-worth into monetary value and hypersexualization.
- Skyrocketing mental health crises, depression, anxiety, and suicide rates.

This isn't just opinion—it's reflected in national health statistics, rising crime, fractured families, and political instability. When God is removed, chaos fills the void.

THE CALL TO REJOICE

Christians, lift your heads. You are not to be mocked or shamed. You are part of the truth, saved by grace, and upheld by the love of the eternal King. Let the world rage; your soul is anchored in the One who conquered death. Rejoice in your faith, for your life has eternal purpose, and your truth will never pass away.

45

The Calling and the Commission

BECOMING A CHRISTIAN is not a mark of weakness, shame, or blind tradition. It is a declaration of truth, strength, and eternal hope. For those who choose Jesus Christ, life begins anew with meaning, purpose, and the indwelling presence of the Holy Spirit. To be a Christian is to walk in truth and in the light of God's love, shielded from the lies of the world and protected from the schemes of Satan.

According to Scripture, a true Christian—one filled with the Holy Spirit—cannot be possessed by the devil. As 1 John 4:4 reminds us, "You, dear children, are from God and have overcome them, because the one who is in you is greater than the one who is in the world." And again, in 2 Cor 6:16, "What agreement is there between the temple of God and idols? For we are the temple of the living God." These verses affirm that those sealed with the Spirit of God are not subject to possession by any unclean spirit.

We live in a time where many have walked away from God's truth. The results are visible: the rise of confusion, identity crises, moral decay, and spiritual emptiness. The modern world, in its rebellion, has turned truth into opinion and perversion into pride. Young children are subjected to gender ideology, and dangerous medical interventions are endorsed as liberation. Social platforms have elevated greed over grace and profit over purpose—young women encouraged to exchange dignity for exploitation. We are not evolving; we are regressing, morally and spiritually.

But there is hope. That hope is found in Jesus Christ. His teachings, when followed, bring healing to families, peace to nations, and dignity to individuals. The gospel offers transformation not by force, but by love and truth.

Let us also remember the legacy of those who came before us—our fathers, grandfathers, and great-grandfathers. These were men and women who stood bravely for their faith, even in the face of war, poverty, or persecution. They built not only churches but entire societies based on Christian values. They founded hospitals, schools, orphanages, and charities. They built the moral and economic structures of our nations by following Christ's call to love, serve, and build.

In the nineteenth and twentieth centuries, many of the greatest universities—Harvard, Yale, Princeton—were founded by Christians to spread the gospel and educate people in truth.

The Red Cross, founded by Henry Dunant, was inspired by his Christian beliefs.

William Wilberforce, a Christian, led the charge in abolishing the British slave trade.

Florence Nightingale, the founder of modern nursing, was a devout Christian who believed her work was a calling from God.

Countless missionaries brought education, medicine, and clean water to remote parts of the world out of love for Christ.

Our freedom today was bought not just with blood but with faith. And now, in our generation, we are called to defend and rebuild what others died to protect: the truth of the gospel.

Christianity is not outdated—it is eternal. It is the anchor of justice, peace, and hope. Do not be ashamed. Rejoice that you carry the truth. Stand boldly for what is right. For the world needs the gospel now more than ever.

> If God is for us, who can be against us? (Rom 8:31)

46

The Road Ahead
What Will You Choose?

FROM THE GARDEN OF Eden to the empty tomb of Christ, from ancient scrolls to artificial intelligence, from the rise and fall of empires to the quiet questions within each human soul—this story is not just God's story. It is your story too.

You, reader, were born into a war. Not a war of politics or nations, but a cosmic war between truth and lies, light and darkness, humility and pride, God and Lucifer.

Throughout this book, you have seen:

- The fingerprints of God on creation.
- The philosophical and historical weight of Jesus's life, death, and resurrection.
- The distortion of truth by false teachings and counterfeit revelations.
- The resilience of the church and the unmistakable power of the gospel.

But now, the final question remains: What will you do with all of this?

The Road Ahead

Will you live for truth, or for comfort? Will you follow the narrow path of faith, or remain in the wide stream of passive ignorance? Will you prepare as if Jesus could return tomorrow, or dismiss it as ancient fiction?

The gospel is not a philosophy to be admired. It is a call to surrender. Jesus said, "Repent, for the kingdom of heaven has come near" (Matt 4:17). That repentance is not just sorrow for sin—it is the conscious turning of one's heart toward truth, toward Christ.

And to follow Christ is not weakness. It is the highest form of strength. In a world where lies are popular and evil is celebrated, it takes immense courage to choose righteousness. It takes vision to see past the temporary pleasures of the flesh. It takes faith to walk forward when the world walks away.

Look around. See how the world is spiraling. Morality is traded for money. Truth is blurred by ideology. Children are confused. Justice is manipulated. Yet even in this chaos, there is a clear light shining—the gospel of Jesus Christ, unchanged, unshaken, and undefeated.

Will you join this eternal story? Will you take your place among those who chose truth over comfort, and eternity over momentary gain?

Because whether you are a scholar or a child, a builder or a teacher, a sinner or a saint—God is calling you. Not just to believe in him, but to walk with him. To be part of his unstoppable plan. To be his. Not because you are perfect, but because he is.

This book was written not to prove how much I know, but to show you how much God knows you. And loves you. And is waiting for you.

Let today be the day you answer that call.

Let this be the day you say, "Here I am, Lord. I choose truth. I choose you."

Final Appendices and Reader Tools

FOOTNOTES AND SOURCE REFERENCES

THROUGHOUT THIS BOOK, MANY quotes and historical references are taken from the Bible, the Qur'an, and well-documented historical events. Below are a few key sources that you can verify:

Biblical References

Jesus and the temple: John 2:19—"Destroy this temple, and I will raise it again in three days"

Satan tempting Jesus: Matt 4:1–11

Jesus and the Father are one: John 10:30

Jesus is the way, the truth, and the life: John 14:6

Repentance and salvation: Luke 13:3, Acts 2:38, Rom 10:9

Tree of life and tree of knowledge: Gen 2:9; 3:22–24

Qur'anic References

Jesus creates a bird from clay: Q 3:49

Jesus did not die (Islamic claim): Q 4:157–58

Jesus is called the Word and Spirit of God: Q 4:171

Mary is honored: Q 19

Allah is the best of planners: Q 3:54

Historical Events

Destruction of the First and Second Temples: 586 BCE (Babylonians), 70 CE (Romans)

Church of the Holy Sepulchre built under Constantine: ca. 325 CE

Sir Lionel Luckhoo on Jesus: Known public record, referenced in apologetics and historical analysis

Rise of Islam and Muhammad's military campaigns: Documented in the Hadith and early Islamic histories

GLOSSARY OF KEY TERMS

Messiah: The anointed one promised in the Hebrew Scriptures. Christians believe this is Jesus.

Temple Mount: The holiest site in Judaism and also important to Islam.

Third Temple: A future Jewish temple anticipated in eschatology.

Jihad: In Islamic context, struggle or holy war.

Crucifixion and resurrection: Central Christian belief of Jesus's death and return to life.

Antichrist: A figure representing opposition to Christ in Christian end-times prophecy.

GOSPEL TIMELINE OVERVIEW

1. Old Testament era: Prophecies and the fall of Israel
2. Jesus's birth: Fulfillment of prophecies, ca. 4–6 BCE
3. Jesus's ministry: Teachings, miracles, ca. 30–33 CE

Final Appendices and Reader Tools

4. Crucifixion and resurrection: 33 CE
5. Temple destroyed by Rome: 70 CE
6. Spread of Christianity: First through Rome, then the world
7. Rise of Islam: ca. 610 CE
8. Modern conflict in Israel: Ongoing, tied to eschatological expectations

INDEX OF KEY TOPICS

Jesus and his divinity, chs. 6, 7, 37

Qur'anic contradictions, chs. 7, 12

Jewish rejection of the Messiah, ch. 8

Satan and the battle for souls, chs. 9, 22

History of the temple, chs. 1, 4, 10

Role of the church in human progress, ch. 16

Modern political prophecy, chs. 32, 36

How to repent, ch. 30

    This reference section is meant to help readers better grasp the historical, theological, and prophetic journey explored in this book. If you're reading with curiosity, or even skepticism, may this be a light in your search for truth.

Bibliography

Bruce, F. F. *Israel and the Nations: The History of Israel from the Exodus to the Fall of the Second Temple*. Revised by David F. Payne. Downers Grove, IL: IVP Academic, 1998.

Darwin, Charles. *The Origin of Species*. Edited by Charles W. Eliot. Harvard Classics. Danbury, CT: Grolier, 1981.

Josephus. *Jewish Antiquities*. In *The Works of Josephus: Complete and Unabridged*, translated by William Whiston, 27–542. Peabody, MA: Hendrickson, 1987.

Lewis, C. S. *The Problem of Pain*. New York: Touchstone, 1996.

Luckhoo, Lionel. *Is There Really Life After Death?* London: Christian Evidence Society, 1984.

Roberts, C. H., ed. *An Unpublished Fragment of the Fourth Gospel in the John Rylands Library*. Manchester: Manchester University Press, 1935.

Tacitus. *The Annals of Imperial Rome*. Translated by Michael Grant. Penguin Classics. London: Penguin, 1996.

Vermes, Geza. *The Complete Dead Sea Scrolls in English*. Rev. ed. Penguin Classics. London: Penguin, 2011.

www.ingramcontent.com/pod-product-compliance
Lightning Source LLC
Chambersburg PA
CBHW071212160426
43196CB00011B/2276